First World War
and Army of Occupation
War Diary
France, Belgium and Germany

18 DIVISION
Divisional Troops
85 Brigade Royal Field Artillery
20 July 1915 - 3 December 1916

WO95/2025/3

The Naval & Military Press Ltd
www.nmarchive.com
Published in association with The National Archives

Published by

The Naval & Military Press Ltd

Unit 10 Ridgewood Industrial Park,

Uckfield, East Sussex,

TN22 5QE England

Tel: +44 (0) 1825 749494

www.naval-military-press.com

www.nmarchive.com

This diary has been reprinted in facsimile from the original. Any imperfections are inevitably reproduced and the quality may fall short of modern type and cartographic standards.

© **Crown Copyright**
Images reproduced by permission of The National Archives, London, England, 2015.

Contents

Document type	Place/Title	Date From	Date To
Heading	WO95/2025 18 Division Divisional Troops 85 Brigade Royal Field Artillery Jul 1915-Dec 1916		
Heading	18th Division 85th Brigade R.F.A. Jly 1915-Dec 1916		
Heading	18th Division 85th Bde R.F.A. Vol I from 25 Jly To 31 Aug 15 Dec 16		
War Diary	Heytesbury Southampton	25/07/1915	25/07/1915
War Diary	Havre	26/07/1915	27/07/1915
War Diary	Amiens Vaux	28/07/1915	28/07/1915
War Diary	Beaucourt	08/08/1915	23/08/1915
War Diary	Bonnay	23/08/1915	31/08/1915
Heading	18th Division "A"/85 Battery R.F.A. Vol. I 25-31-7-15		
War Diary	Heytesbury	25/07/1915	25/07/1915
War Diary	Havre	26/07/1915	27/07/1915
War Diary	Vaux Des Amienoise	28/07/1915	31/07/1915
Heading	18th Division "A"/85 Battery R.F.A. Vol. II From 1-29.8.15		
War Diary	Vaux En Amienoise	01/08/1915	07/08/1915
War Diary	Beacourt Sur L'Hallue	08/08/1915	23/08/1915
War Diary	Bonnay	23/08/1915	31/08/1915
War Diary		27/08/1915	29/08/1915
Heading	18th Division B/85 Battery Vol I July 15		
Heading	War Diary of 'B' Battery 85th Bde R.F.A. From 24th July To 31st July 1915 (Volume I)		
War Diary	Heytesbury Wilts	24/07/1915	25/07/1915
War Diary	Warminster Wilts	25/07/1915	25/07/1915
War Diary	Southampton	25/07/1915	25/07/1915
War Diary	France Havre	26/07/1915	26/07/1915
War Diary	Havre	27/07/1915	27/07/1915
War Diary	Longeau	28/07/1915	28/07/1915
War Diary	Vaux-En-Amienois	28/07/1915	28/07/1915
War Diary	France Vaux	28/07/1915	28/07/1915
Heading	18th Division B/85 Battery Vol 2 August 15		
Heading	War Diary of 'B' Battery 85th Bde RFA From 1st August To 31st August 1915 Volume II		
War Diary	France	01/08/1915	01/08/1915
War Diary	Vaux-En Amienois Beaucourt	08/08/1915	08/08/1915
War Diary	Ville-Sur L'Ancre	19/08/1915	24/08/1915
War Diary	France	24/08/1915	24/08/1915
Diagram etc	Plan		
Diagram etc	Section AA		
Heading	18th Division "C"/85 Battery Vol. I July & Aug 1-15		
War Diary		20/07/1915	31/08/1915
Diagram etc	A Gun Emplacement Section AA		
Diagram etc	A Gun Emplacement Ground Plan		
Heading	18th Division "D"/85 Battery R.F.A. Vol. I From 25th Jly to 31 Aug 15		
Miscellaneous	D Battery 88th (Hors") Bde RFA		
War Diary	Heytesbury	25/07/1915	25/07/1915
War Diary	Southampton	25/07/1915	25/07/1915
War Diary	Havre	26/07/1915	27/07/1915

War Diary	Vaux	28/07/1915	29/07/1915
War Diary	Mericourt L'Abbe	29/07/1915	30/07/1915
War Diary	Mericourt	31/07/1915	01/08/1915
War Diary	Martinsart	02/08/1915	31/08/1915
Heading	18th Div 85th Bde AC Vol 1,2,3,4,5 Aug		
Heading	War Diary of 85th B.A.C R.F.A. from 1st August-31 August 1915 Vol 1		
War Diary	Bonnay	23/08/1915	25/08/1915
War Diary	Treux	28/08/1915	31/08/1915
Heading	War Diary of 85th BAC-R.F.A. from 1st September to 30th September 1915 Vol 2		
War Diary	Treux	01/09/1915	30/09/1915
Heading	War Diary of 85th B.A.C. R.F.A. from 1st October 31st October 1915 Vol 3		
War Diary	Treux	01/10/1915	30/10/1915
Heading	War Diary of 85th B.A.C. R.F.A. from 1st November-30th November 1915 Vol 4		
War Diary	Treux	01/11/1915	30/11/1915
Heading	War Diary of 85th B.A.C. R.F.A. from 1st December To 31st Dec Vol 5		
War Diary	Treux	01/12/1915	31/12/1915
Heading	18th Division A/85 Battery R.F.A. Vol 3 Sept. 15		
War Diary	Bonnay	01/09/1915	01/09/1915
War Diary	Ville Sur L'Ancre	02/09/1915	04/09/1915
War Diary	Becordel	05/09/1915	19/09/1915
War Diary	Albert	20/09/1915	20/09/1915
War Diary	Becordel	20/09/1915	21/09/1915
War Diary	Albert	23/09/1915	30/09/1915
Heading	18th Division B/85 Battery Vol 3 4 5 Oct Nov Sept 15		
Heading	War Diary of 'B' Battery 85th Bde R.F.A. From 1st September To 30th Sept 1915 Volume III		
War Diary	Bray Sur-Somme	01/09/1915	08/09/1915
War Diary	Ville-Sur L'Ancre To Meaulte	18/09/1915	18/09/1915
War Diary	Bray	21/09/1915	21/09/1915
Heading	War Diary of 'B' Battery 85th Bde R.F.A. From 1st October To 31st Oct 1915 Volume IV		
War Diary	France Bray-Sur-Somme	01/10/1915	26/10/1915
War Diary	Meaulte	01/10/1915	01/10/1915
Heading	War Diary of 'B' Battery 85th Bde R.F.A. From 1st November To 30th Nov 1915 (Volume V)		
War Diary	France Bray Sur Somme	01/11/1915	01/11/1915
War Diary	Meaulte	01/12/1915	01/12/1915
Heading	18th Division C/85 Battery Vol 2 Sep 1-15		
Heading	Herewith the War Diary of C/85 RFA for the Month of September		
War Diary		01/09/1915	25/09/1915
Heading	18th Div C/85 Battery RFA Vol 3 Sept		
War Diary	Meaulte	01/09/1915	31/12/1915
Heading	18th Division D/85 Battery R.F.A. Vol II Sep 1-15		
War Diary	Martinsart	01/09/1915	30/09/1915
Heading	85th Bde. R.F.A. Vols 2 3 Oct 15		
Heading	War Diary of 85th Brigade R.F.A. Hd Q. From 1.9.15 To 30.9.15 Vol 1		
War Diary	Bonnay	02/09/1915	02/09/1915
War Diary	Ville-Sur-Ancre	02/09/1915	04/09/1915
War Diary	Treux	18/09/1915	30/09/1915

Heading	War Diary of 85th Brigade R.F.A. Hd Qr From 1.10.15 To 31.10.15 (Vol 2)		
War Diary	Treux	01/10/1915	31/10/1915
Heading	18th Division A/85 Battery R.F.A. Vol 4 Oct 15		
War Diary	Albert	01/10/1915	31/10/1915
War Diary		02/10/1915	26/10/1915
Heading	18th Division D/85 Battery R.F.A. Vol 3 Oct 15		
War Diary	Martinsart	01/10/1915	31/10/1915
Heading	18th Division 85th Bde R.F.A. Vol 4 Nov 15		
Heading	War Diary of 85th Brigade R.F.A. From 1st November To 30th November 1915 Vol 1		
War Diary	Treux	01/11/1915	30/11/1915
Heading	18th Division D/85 Battery R.F.A. Vol 4 Nov. 15		
War Diary	Martinsart	01/11/1915	30/11/1915
Heading	18th Div 85th Bde. R.F.A. Vol. 5 Dec		
Heading	War Diary of 85th Brigade R.F.A. From 1.12.1915 To 31.12.1915 Volume II		
War Diary	Treux	01/12/1915	31/12/1915
Heading	18th A/85 Battery R.F.A. Vol 6 Dec		
War Diary	Albert	01/12/1915	31/12/1915
Heading	18th Division B/85 Battery Vol 6 Dec 15		
Heading	War Diary of 'B' Battery 85th Bde R.F.A. From 1st December To 31st Dec 1915 (Volume VI)		
War Diary	France Bray-Sur Somme	01/12/1915	29/12/1915
War Diary	Meaulte	01/12/1915	01/12/1915
Heading	18th Division D/85 Battery Vol 5 Dec 15		
War Diary	Martinsart	01/12/1915	08/12/1915
War Diary	Martinsart & Aveluy	09/12/1915	22/12/1915
War Diary	Martinsart	23/12/1915	31/12/1915
Miscellaneous	Report On Fire Cutting at R. 31 C 30 by a Single 4.5 Hours on 15.12.15	15/12/1915	15/12/1915
Miscellaneous	B Report On Wire Cutting carried out by a Single 4.5 Howitzer II/85 R.F.A.		
Miscellaneous	Gunnery Notes		
Heading	85th Bde RFA Vol 6 Jan 16		
Heading	War Diary of 85th Brigade R.F.A. Hd Qr From 1st Jan 1916 To 31.1.16 Vol III		
War Diary	Treux	01/01/1916	30/01/1916
Heading	B/85 Battery Vol 7 Jan		
Heading	War Diary of B Battery 85th Bde R.F.A. From 1st January 1916 To 31st January 1916 (Volume VII)		
War Diary	Bray-Sur Somme	01/01/1916	31/01/1916
War Diary	Meaulte	01/01/1916	30/01/1916
Heading	C/85 Battery Vol 4 Jan		
Heading	C 85 R.F.A. Jan Vol		
War Diary	Meaulte	04/01/1916	31/01/1916
Heading	D/85 Battery R.F.A. Vol 6 Jan 16		
War Diary	Martinsart	01/01/1916	18/01/1916
War Diary	Warloy Baillon	19/01/1916	20/01/1916
War Diary	Buire	21/01/1916	31/01/1916
Heading	War Diary of 85th Brigade R.F.A. Hd Qr From 1.2.16 To 29.2.16 Volume (IV)		
War Diary	Treux	01/02/1916	01/02/1916
War Diary	Lavieville	03/02/1916	29/02/1916
Heading	A Bty 85th Bde R.F.A. Vol IV		
War Diary	Albert	01/02/1916	29/02/1916

Heading	B. Battery 85th Bde R.F.A. 18 Div Vol 8		
Heading	War Diary of 'B' Battery 85th Bde R.F.A. From 1st February To 29th Feb 1916 (Volume VIII)		
War Diary			
War Diary	France Bray-Sur Somme	01/02/1916	01/02/1916
War Diary	Meaulte	02/02/1916	02/02/1916
War Diary	Bray-Sur Somme	06/02/1916	07/02/1916
War Diary	Buire-Sur L'Ancre	08/02/1916	08/02/1916
War Diary	Talmas	09/02/1916	09/02/1916
War Diary	France Fransu	09/02/1916	11/02/1916
War Diary	Halloy	12/02/1916	12/02/1916
War Diary	Couturelle	14/02/1916	16/02/1916
War Diary	Monchiet	16/02/1916	24/02/1916
Heading	C. Batt 85th R.F.A. 18th Div Vol 5 Feb		
War Diary	Meaulte	04/02/1916	07/02/1916
War Diary	Lavieville	12/02/1916	29/02/1916
War Diary	Buire	01/02/1916	02/02/1916
War Diary	Meaulte	03/02/1916	29/02/1916
Heading	85 R.F.A. Mar Vol 8		
War Diary	Meaulte	01/03/1916	03/03/1916
War Diary	Bresle	04/03/1916	04/03/1916
War Diary	Bossy	05/03/1916	09/03/1916
War Diary	Suzanne	10/03/1916	31/03/1916
War Diary	Lavieville	01/03/1916	03/03/1916
War Diary	Bussy Les Daours	03/03/1916	22/03/1916
War Diary	Bray	22/03/1916	31/03/1916
Heading	A/85 R F A Vol 7 Mar		
War Diary	Albert	01/03/1916	02/03/1916
War Diary	Bresle	03/03/1916	03/03/1916
War Diary	Bussy	04/03/1916	09/03/1916
War Diary	Maricourt	09/03/1916	31/03/1916
Heading	85 RFA C/Batt Vol 6 Mar		
War Diary	Lavieville	01/03/1916	30/03/1916
Heading	War Diary of 85 Brigade R.F.A. Hd. Qrs From 1.4.16 To 30.4.16 Vol V		
War Diary			
War Diary	Maricourt	01/04/1916	29/04/1916
War Diary	120 MM Wood Near Vaux Near Suzanne	09/04/1916	22/04/1916
War Diary		19/04/1916	21/04/1916
War Diary		19/04/1916	19/04/1916
War Diary	Suzanne	30/04/1916	30/04/1916
War Diary		29/04/1916	29/04/1916
War Diary		25/04/1916	26/04/1916
War Diary	Suzanne	01/04/1916	30/04/1916
War Diary	Bray Sur Somme	01/04/1916	30/04/1916
Heading	War Diary of 85 Bde R.F.A. Hd Q From 1.5.16 To 31.5.16 Vol II		
War Diary	Bray Sur Somme	01/05/1916	01/05/1916
War Diary	Bray	06/05/1916	06/05/1916
War Diary	Bois Des Tailles	06/05/1916	31/05/1916
War Diary	North West of Bray	25/05/1916	31/05/1916
War Diary	North West of Bray	01/06/1916	30/06/1916
Heading	War Diary of 85th Brigade RFA Hd Qrs From 1.6.16 To 30.6.16 Vol VII		
War Diary	Bois Des Tailles	01/06/1916	30/06/1916
Heading	War Diary of 85th Brigade R.F.A. From 1.7.16 31.7.16		

War Diary	Bois Des Tailles	01/07/1916	12/07/1916
War Diary	N of Billon Wood	17/07/1916	20/07/1916
War Diary	Billon Wood	21/07/1916	21/07/1916
War Diary	Northern Bois De Failles	22/07/1916	22/07/1916
War Diary	Querrieu	23/07/1916	23/07/1916
War Diary	Allery	24/07/1916	27/07/1916
War Diary	Caestre	28/07/1916	28/07/1916
Heading	War Diary of 85 Brigade R.F.A. From 1.8.16 31.8.16 Vol IX		
War Diary	Eecke & Caestre	01/08/1916	02/08/1916
War Diary	South of Bois Grenier	03/08/1916	25/08/1916
War Diary	N.W. of Croix Du Bac	27/08/1916	29/08/1916
War Diary	Authieule	30/08/1916	30/08/1916
War Diary	Vadencourt	31/08/1916	31/08/1916
Heading	War Diary of 85 Brigade R.F.A. From 1.9.16 To 30.9.16 Vol X		
War Diary	Brickfields 1/2 Mile NW Albert	01/09/1916	03/09/1916
War Diary	Contalmaison	04/09/1916	30/09/1916
Heading	War Diary of 85th Brigade R.F.A. From 1.10.16 To 31.10.16 Vol XI		
War Diary	Becourt Wood	01/10/1916	01/10/1916
War Diary	Authville Wood	02/10/1916	08/10/1916
War Diary	Mesnil	09/10/1916	31/10/1916
Heading	War Diary For November 1916 85th Bde R.F.A. Vol 16		
Heading	War Diary of 85th Brigade R.F.A. From 1.11.16 To 3.12.16 Vol XI		
War Diary	Mesnil	01/11/1916	03/12/1916

WO 95/2025

(3) 18 Division
Divisional Troops.

85 Brigade Royal Field
Artillery

Jul 1915 - Dec 1916

16TH DIVISION

85TH BRIGADE R.F.A.
JLY 1915-DEC 1916

BROKEN UP

12/6607

18th Division

86th Bde: R.F.A.
Vol: I.

From 25 July to 31 Aug. 15

Dec 16

Army Form C. 2118

85 "Bde R.F.A"

WAR DIARY
or
INTELLIGENCE SUMMARY
(Erase heading not required.)

Instructions regarding War Diaries and Intelligence Summaries are contained in F.S. Regs., Part II. and the Staff Manual respectively. Title Pages will be prepared in manuscript.

Place	Date	Hour	Summary of Events and Information	Remarks and references to Appendices
Heytesbury	25.7.15	9 a.m.	85" Bde R.F.A left HEYTESBURY	[sgd]
Southampton	"	8 p.m.	Left SOUTHAMPTON for France	[sgd]
Havre	26 "	3 a.m.	Arrived HAVRE	[sgd]
"	"	5 p.m.	REST CAMP No 5	[sgd]
"	27 "	12 noon	Left HAVRE	[sgd]
Amiens	28 "	12.30 a.m.	Arrived AMIENS - detrained and commenced journey to new billeting area by road	[sgd]
Vaux	28 "	8.30 a.m.	Arrived VAUX (small village) - only troops there.	[sgd]
"	29 "		T/85 left Vaux for attachment to 51st T/B which was in action	[sgd]
"	28.15	2.30 p.m.	H.Q. A, B, & A/c inspected by Corps Comdr	[sgd]
"	"		6/85 left Vaux for attachment to 5th Divn	[sgd]
"	"		2 subsections 85 B.A.C. left for Vaux, one to go with C/85, the other T/85	[sgd]
Beaucourt	18.8.15	5 p.m.	Bde H.Q, A.B. & A/c left for BEAUCOURT, a distance from VAUX & Latour 12 miles (Village slightly larger than VAUX)	[sgd]
"	19th		B/85 left BEAUCOURT for attachment to 82nd Bde R.F.A. (187th)	[sgd]
"	23rd	7/6 a.m.	Left BEAUCOURT for BONNAY (a small timbered-down village)	[sgd]
Bonnay	23rd	8.15 a.m.	Arrived BONNAY - Bde Comdr Area Commandant - Area comprised (since his Bde) 18" T.M.C. (Forty), one Heavy Bam and an H.S.C. Company	[sgd]
"	25 "	7.30 a.m.	1/2 A/c 85" left BEAUCOURT - one subsection for attachment to 13/5, the other to TREUX	[sgd]
"	26 "		H.Q & A/85 only left in BONNAY intact	[sgd]

1875 Wt. W593/826 1,000,000 4/15 J.B.C. & A. A.D.S.S./Forms/C. 2118.

Army Form C. 2118

WAR DIARY
or
INTELLIGENCE SUMMARY

(Erase heading not required.)

Instructions regarding War Diaries and Intelligence Summaries are contained in F.S. Regs., Part II. and the Staff Manual respectively. Title Pages will be prepared in manuscript.

Place	Date	Hour	Summary of Events and Information	Remarks and references to Appendices
BONN AR	31/8/15		H.Q. 4A/185 54th at BONN AR	PSW

121/6300

18th Division

"A"/85 Battery RFA.
Vol. I
25-3-15 — 7-1-15

WARDIARY
or
INTELLIGENCE SUMMARY

Army Form C. 2118

Place	Date	Hour	Summary of Events and Information	Remarks and references to Appendices
HEYTESBURY	25.7.15	8.30 a.m. 9.30 a.m.	Marched by ½ Batteries at two stations to WARMINSTER, Entrained in two trains which started at 11.25 a.m. and 12.35 p.m. for SOUTHAMPTON. Strength:— MAJOR A. THORP Commanding LIEUT. A. R. FINNIS 2ⁿᵈ LT C. R. FENTON " A. S. AVERILL BSM. (W.O.) J.D. VOAK. 130 Other ranks (including 2 A.S.C. drivers) 123 Horses 4 4.5" Howitzers 8 Amm: Wagons 2 G.S. Wagons, 1 Water Cart & 1 Mess Cart Embarked partly in S.S. "Courtfield" and partly in S.S. "Munich"	
HAVRE	26.7.15		Disembarked at HAVRE and went into camp No 3. Increase 2 Light Draught Horses.	
"	27.7.15		Entrained Gare des Marchandise and left at 11.55 a.m. Decrease 1 R: and 1 L.D. Horse Arrived AMIENS, detrained and left station at 11.15 p.m.	

Army Form C. 2118

WAR DIARY
or
INTELLIGENCE SUMMARY
(Erase heading not required.)

Instructions regarding War Diaries and Intelligence Summaries are contained in F.S. Regs., Part II. and the Staff Manual respectively. Title Pages will be prepared in manuscript.

Place	Date	Hour	Summary of Events and Information	Remarks and references to Appendices
VAUX DES AMIENOISE	28.7.15	7.30 a.m.	Arrived and went into billets	
"	29.7.15		Remained in billets	
"	30.7.15		— do —	
"	31.7.15		— do —	

A Sharp
MAJOR, R.F.A.
COMDG 'A'/85th BRIGADE R.F.A.

18th Division

12/6607

"A"/85 Battery R.F.A.
Vol: II
From 1-29.8.16

WAR DIARY or INTELLIGENCE SUMMARY

Army Form C. 2118

Place	Date	Hour	Summary of Events and Information	Remarks and references to Appendices
VAUX EN AMIENOISE	1.8.15		Changed billets to others in same village, lately occupied by D/51-RFA	
"	2.8.15		Remained in billets	
"	3.8.15		— do —	
"	4.8.15		— do —	
"	5.8.15		— do — Inspected by Lieut Gen Morland Comdg X Army Corps 5.12 pm	
"	6.8.15		Decrease 1 R: and 1 L.D. Horse to Mobile Veterinary Section. Remained in billets	
"	7.8.15		Remained in billets. Decrease 1 R: Horse to Mobile Veterinary Section.	
BEAUCOURT SUR L'HALLUE	8.8.15 to 23.8.15	8.30 pm	Marched 5.30 pm V Vaux into billets Remained in billets. Temp/ Lt J.B. Parker attached to battery from 16.8.15	
BONNAY	23.8.15 to 31.8.15	9.15 AM	Marched 7 pm V Vaux into billets Remained in billets.	
	27.8.15		Decrease 1 Gunner accidentally wounded	
	28.8.15		Increase 1 S.Smith 1 Gunner Y 2 Drivers joined from Base Horses	
	29.8.15		Increase 1 R: and 3 L.D. Horses.	

W Shophogon R.H.
Capt A/51 Bee R.F.A

18th K wacun

B/85 Battery
Vol I

121/7795

July 15

CONFIDENTIAL

WAR DIARY

of

'B' BATTERY 85TH BDE R.F.A.

FROM 24TH JULY TO 31ST JULY 1915.

(VOLUME I.)

Army Form C. 2118

WAR DIARY
or
INTELLIGENCE SUMMARY

"B" Batty 85th Bde
R.F.A.

(Erase heading not required.)

Instructions regarding War Diaries and Intelligence Summaries are contained in F.S. Regs., Part II. and the Staff Manual respectively. Title Pages will be prepared in manuscript.

Place	Date 1915	Hour	Summary of Events and Information	Remarks and references to Appendices
HEYTESBURY, WILTS.	24/VII/1915	11.45 pm	Half Battery paraded and marched by road to WARMINSTER, WILTS.	J.J.
	25/VII	1.30 a.m.	Remainder of Battery paraded and marched by road to WARMINSTER, WILTS. Surplus stores and barracks were handed over to Officer i/c Base Details.	J.J.
WARMINSTER, WILTS.	25/VII	3.0 a.m.	Entrainment of Battery at WARMINSTER, without special difficulty – Weather was favourable.	J.J.
SOUTHAMPTON	25/VII	7.0 a.m.	Battery detrained at SOUTHAMPTON. Guns and vehicles, stores and horses, were embarked on transport 'COURTFIELD' and also the drivers detailed for these horses. Gunners and remainder of battery were embarked on transport 'MUNICH' Arrangements for embarkation were good and no difficulty was experienced.	J.J.
		8.0 pm	Transport left SOUTHAMPTON. An escort was provided by navy. No occurrence on transports to report.	J.J.

Army Form C. 2118

B Baty 85th Bde
R.F.A.

WAR DIARY
or
INTELLIGENCE SUMMARY
(Erase heading not required.)

Instructions regarding War Diaries and Intelligence Summaries are contained in F.S. Regs., Part II. and the Staff Manual respectively. Title Pages will be prepared in manuscript.

Place	Date 1915	Hour	Summary of Events and Information	Remarks and references to Appendices
FRANCE. HAVRE	26/VII	5.0 a.m.	Arrived at HAVRE	S.I.
		8.0 a.m.	Battery disembarked at HAVRE - no special difficulty being experienced and after disembarking guns, vehicles and stores marched to REST CAMP No.1, HAVRE.	
HAVRE	27/VII	10.0 a.m.	Marched from REST CAMP, HAVRE to GARE DU NORD where the battery entrained on one train, a small detachment of infantry also travelling on the same train - Some difficulty was experienced in entraining a nervous horse but the battery was entrained in good time -	S.I.
		2.0 p.m.	Departure of train from HAVRE.	S.I.
LONGEAU	28/VII	1.0 a.m.	Arrival of train at LONGEAU near AMIENS and detraining of battery which was carried out smoothly	S.I.
VAUX-EN-AMIENOIS	28/VII	7.0 a.m.	The battery then marched, via AMIENS to the village of VAUX-EN-AMIENOIS at this village the battery rejoined the 85th Brigade R.F.A. The weather at this period was fine, occasional showers of rain only being experienced	S.I.

WAR DIARY
or
INTELLIGENCE SUMMARY

"B" Bty. 85th Bde
R.F.A.

Army Form C. 2118

(Erase heading not required.)

Instructions regarding War Diaries and Intelligence Summaries are contained in F. S. Regs., Part II. and the Staff Manual respectively. Title Pages will be prepared in manuscript.

Place	Date 1915	Hour	Summary of Events and Information	Remarks and references to Appendices
FRANCE. VAUX (contd).	28/VII	—	At VAUX the horses and vehicles were billeted in a grassy field on a slight rise overlooking the village, overhead cover from aircraft being provided for by arranging them alongside a hedge and several scattered trees. Men were billeted in the village, the kits being mostly barns with straw beds. Water for drinking was obtained from wells and for animals from the village watering places; the quality of the water was bad and its effect was soon noticed on the health of the horses. Whilst at VAUX the battery carried out training. The specialists were trained in signalling, etc. Gunners received drill to familiarize them with their equipment and the drivers were occupied in exercising their horses. At VAUX the howitzer dial sights and carriers were fully tested by the Brigade Staff Officers. Whilst at VAUX the optical arrangements of the one-man rangefinders (Artillery - Barr & Stroud MkI) were found defective and this instrument was returned to the D.A.D.O.S.	J.N.

18/85 Saltburg
162

12/
7795.

18th Kurraum

August 15

CONFIDENTIAL

WAR DIARY

OF

"B" BATTERY 85TH BDE RFA

FROM 1ST AUGUST TO 31ST AUGUST 1915

(VOLUME II).

Army Form C. 2118

"B" Bty 85th Bde
R.F.A.

WAR DIARY
or
INTELLIGENCE SUMMARY
(Erase heading not required.)

Instructions regarding War Diaries and Intelligence Summaries are contained in F.S. Regs., Part II. and the Staff Manual respectively. Title Pages will be prepared in manuscript.

Place	Date 1915	Hour	Summary of Events and Information	Remarks and references to Appendices
FRANCE VAUX-EN-AMIENOIS	1/VIII	—	At the beginning of this month the battery was at VAUX engaged in training	
BEAUCOURT	5 & 8/VIII	4.30 pm	The battery marched by road from VAUX to BEAUCOURT-SUR-L'HALLUE where horse lines were taken up in an orchard - good overhead cover from observation being obtained. Whilst at BEAUCOURT training was carried on as before. Drinking water was obtained from a spring pitcher and horses were watered at a stream, the water being excellent.	1
VILLE-SUR-L'ANCRE	19/VIII	2.0 pm	Battery marched by road from BEAUCOURT to VILLE-SUR-L'ANCRE taking up a position in the MAIRIE which was suitable, affording good cover from hostile aircraft and providing an excellent water supply for animals. Reconnaissance work was then carried out by officers for suitable gun positions. Billets for men detailed to remain at this Wagon Line, were obtained in a farm at the village of VILLE	3
	24/VIII	—	A working party of gunners, marched via MORLANCOURT to a spinney North of BRAY-SUR-SOMME.	

1875. Wt. W593/826 1,000,000 4/15 J.B.C. & A. A.D.S.S./Forms/C. 2118.

WAR DIARY or ~~INTELLIGENCE SUMMARY~~

'B' Baty 85th Bde R.F.A.

Army Form C. 2118

(Erase heading not required.)

Place	Date	Hour	Summary of Events and Information	Remarks and references to Appendices
FRANCE	24/VIII	—	This opening was made a camp for the party who commenced the construction of gun pits in positions previously selected in a valley about 1 mile N of BRAY. As a precaution against hostile aeroplanes, work was suspended whenever any were observed by a regularly posted picquet. Remainder of the month was occupied in digging the gun pits, no special difficulty being experienced.	

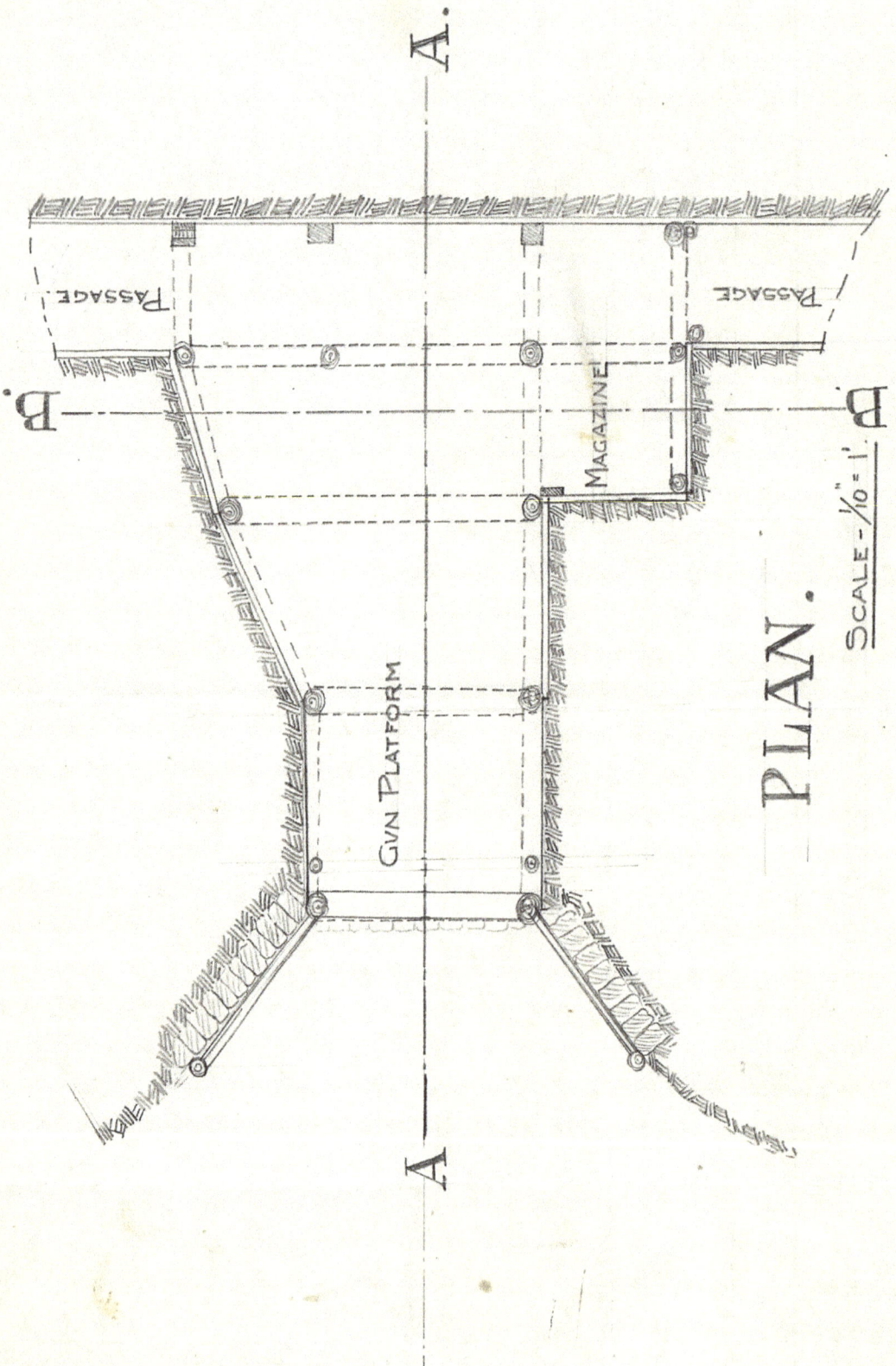

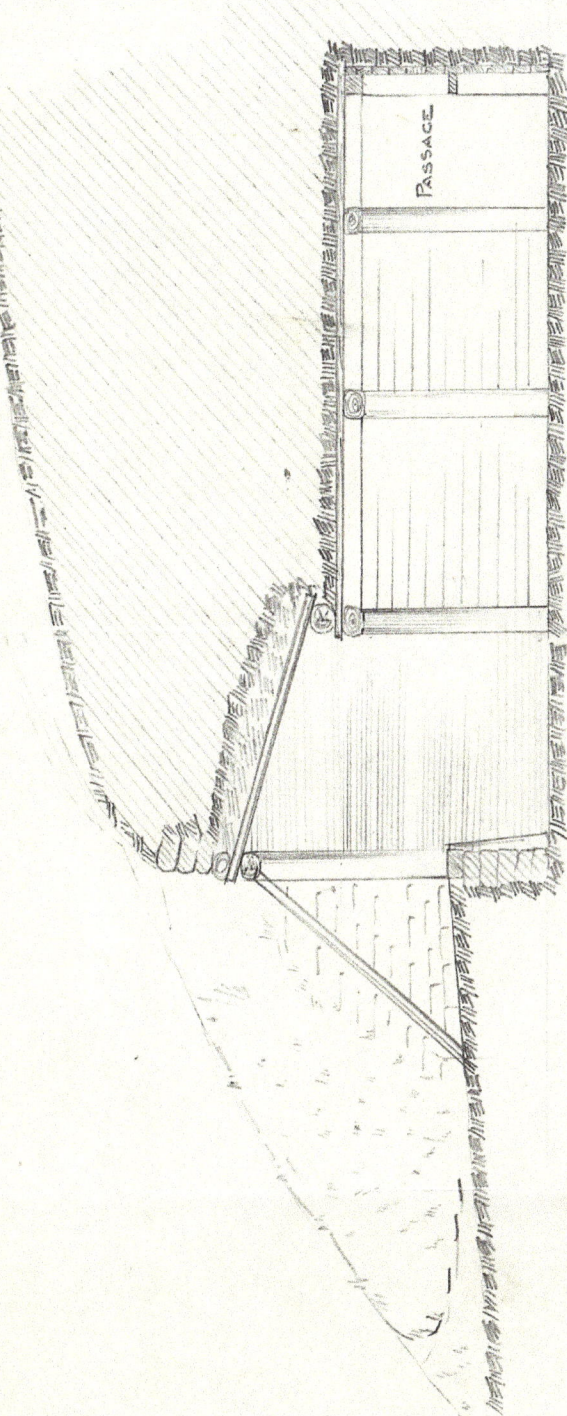

SECTION AA

SCALE — 1/10" = 1'

18th Division

"C"/85 Battery
Vol I
July & August 15

War Diary.
C/85 R.F.A.

20.7.15. Heytesbury. Battery reduced to War Scale.

25.7.15 Battery entrains at 4.30 & 6 am at WARMINSTER, embarks at Southampton, sails at 5 pm for LE

26.7.15 HAVRE, arriving there next morning. On disembarkation, moved to No 5 Rest Camp.

27.7.15 Battery moves by rail to AMIENS thence by road to VAUX-EN-AMIENOIS — went into Billets at VAUX. bad water supply.

2.8.15 After a few days training under battery arrangements, the battery moved by road to HEILLY, bivouacked in excellent wonac by the river, arriving 4.30 pm. attached to 28th Bde 5th Division in Left Group. Cmdr. Col. Sandy.

3.8.15. Position reconnoitred & gun position selected in valley east of MEAULTE. No position to take over as the French had no howitzer battery in the Left Group.

3.8.15 — In the evening the battery moved
up to bivouac & billets at
DERNANCOURT about 3 miles behind
gun position.

4.8.15 — Digging gun pits started.
5.8.15)
6.8.15) digging continued, delayed by lack of
7. ")   material as wood & revetting material
8.8.15 — No 1 gun placed in action
9.8.15. — Other pits continued
10.8.15 Remaining 3 guns put in position
Orders received to readjust ammn.
70% Lyddite 30% Shrapnel.
11.8.15. Gun pits completed & screening
commenced.
12.8.15 Registration commenced. Wagon line moved to W of MEAULTE
Reference Line FRICOURT CHURCH
Points registered pt 479. 498.
                                          HE 21 rounds.
13.8.15 Points registered pt 478, 486 HE rounds
14.8.15 A Section ranged on each of above points
                                          HE 18 rounds
17.8.15 Points registered pt 303 & BOIS
ALLEMAND .   HE 22 round
19.8.15 Points registered pt 477, 955.
2 effective rounds obtained on machine
gun emplacement reported at the left
edge of LA HAIE JOSEPH. Emplacement
not used since.   HE 11 rounds

21.8.15 Registered points 488, 493. Machine gun emplacement reported at 488 this was shelled & the infantry report was satisfactory. 17 HE rds

23.8.15 M.S. received that our trenches on the BOIS Francais were being shelled by trench howitzer, located behind BOIS ALLEMAND. 11 Lyddite allowed observations carried out from trenches on BOIS FRANCAIS. The minenwerfer was silenced & though the german field guns opened fire, the minenwerfer has not fired since (25.8.15) Telephone wire of 122 RFA used through exchange.
11 rds Lyddite

25.8.15 Registered FRICOURT BRIDGE. In the evening registered front trench from BOIS ALLEMAND to point 301, using observations from in front of battery & from flank observer 1500' from tgt at right angle to line to tgt. Rounds reported by infantry to be falling in front trenches opposite. Observation from front trench is almost impossible owing to concave slope & mine craters. 17 rds HE

25th. Plans & sections of gunpits & dug outs constructed by C/85. The drawings by 2/Lt Fish.

Work as shown completed in about 14 days working by daylight & 8 men per gun at a time.

Soil. Surface soil soft mould for 18", under this solid chalk requiring quarrying.

The bearing of bank was 10°, bearing of guns from 40° – 90°, causing the guns to be echeloned. The height of bank varied from 5' – 7'6" in height.

25/26th At midnight on this day the group cmdrs of the 18th Divn took over from 5th Divn. & C/85 came under Left Group Cmdr Col English, cmdg 84th Bde R.F.A.

The absence of unnecessary reports & returns was noticeable while attached to 18th Bde. To other brigades we had to render a return every evening stating our "estimated casualties & expenditure of ammn up to noon of that day". Sent to another brigade, a daily report at 7.30am
A. of no of rounds fired by our artillery
B. no of rounds fired by enemy artillery.

27.8.15 Light very bad. Fired a few rounds at a quarry where Germans cook. Infantry reported that some men were seen bolting.
4 Shrapnel

28.8.15. Visited by Col Wylde Cmdg 85th Bde. Shelled Greyhouse at request of Infantry.
10 HE 6 Shrapnel

30.8.15 Enemys artillery showing more activity. Fired 2 rounds at 10 pm at corner of FRICOURT village to silence a rifle grenade battery reported by E. Surreys.
2 rds HE

31.8.15. Shoot arranged for with aeroplane, but aeroplane came in without any message being sent to open fire. Copy of letter from Genl Kavanagh 5th Division to Genl Mascee Cmdg 18th Division forwarded to battery, complimenting Genl Mascee on the artillery of 18th Divn lent to 5th Division.

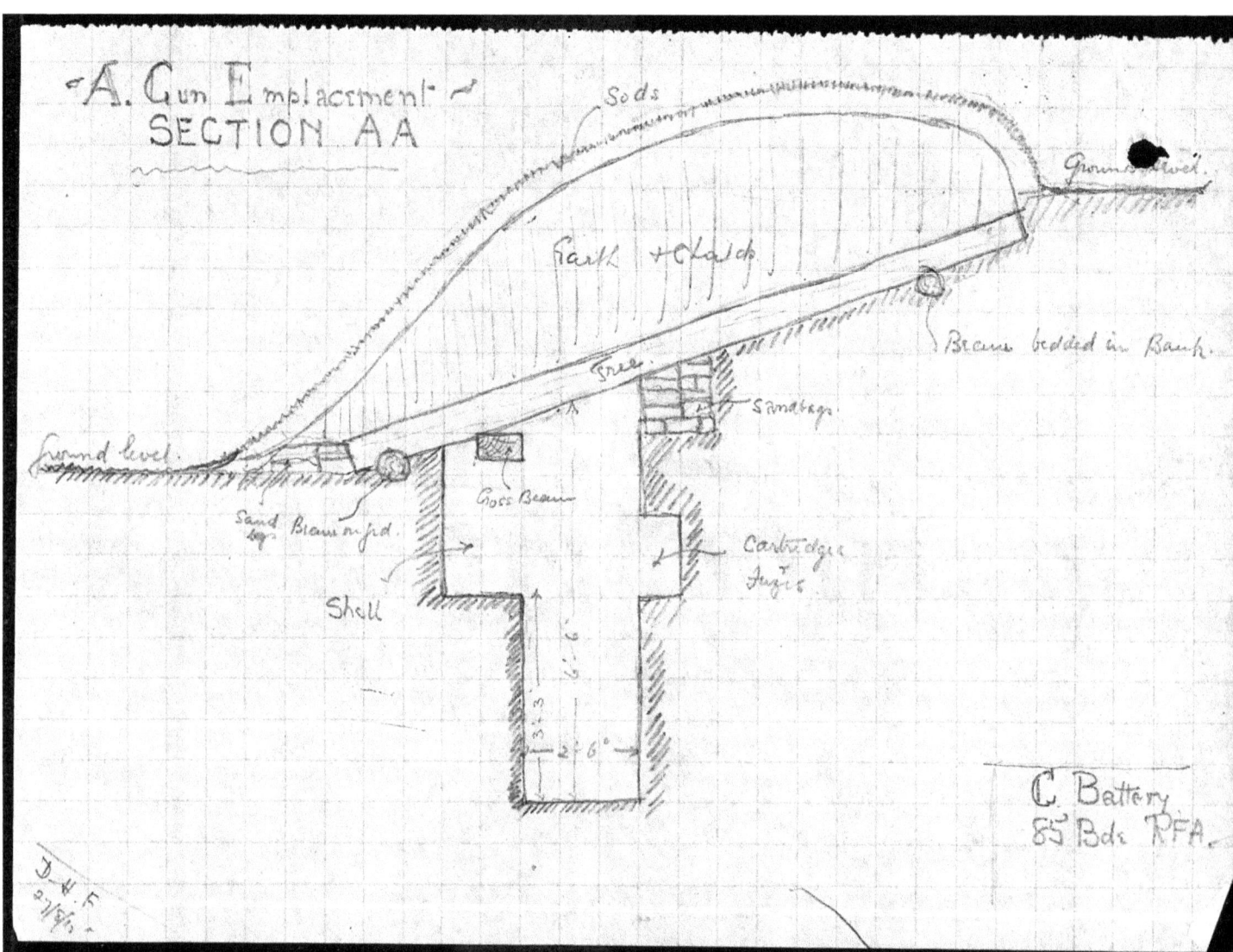

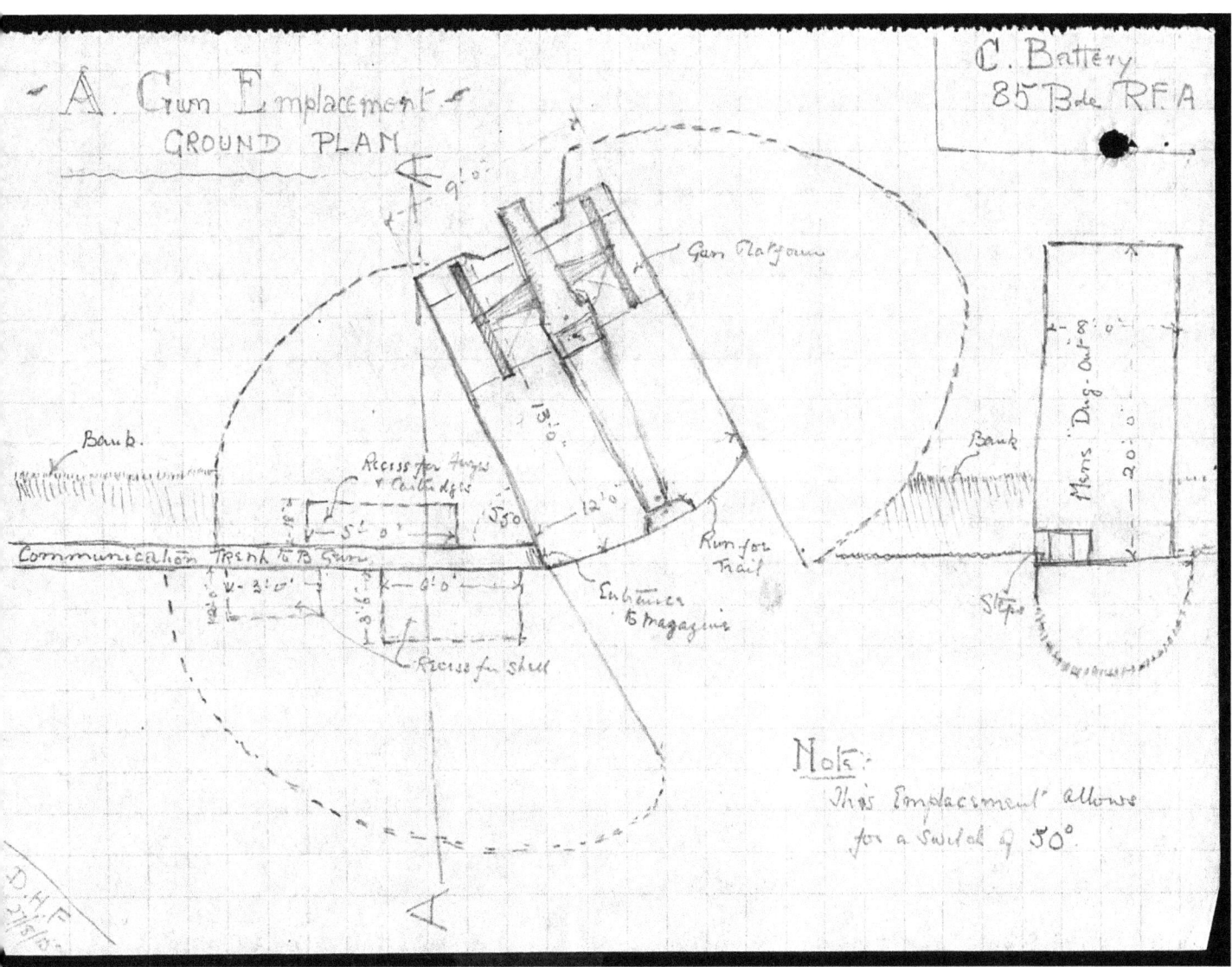

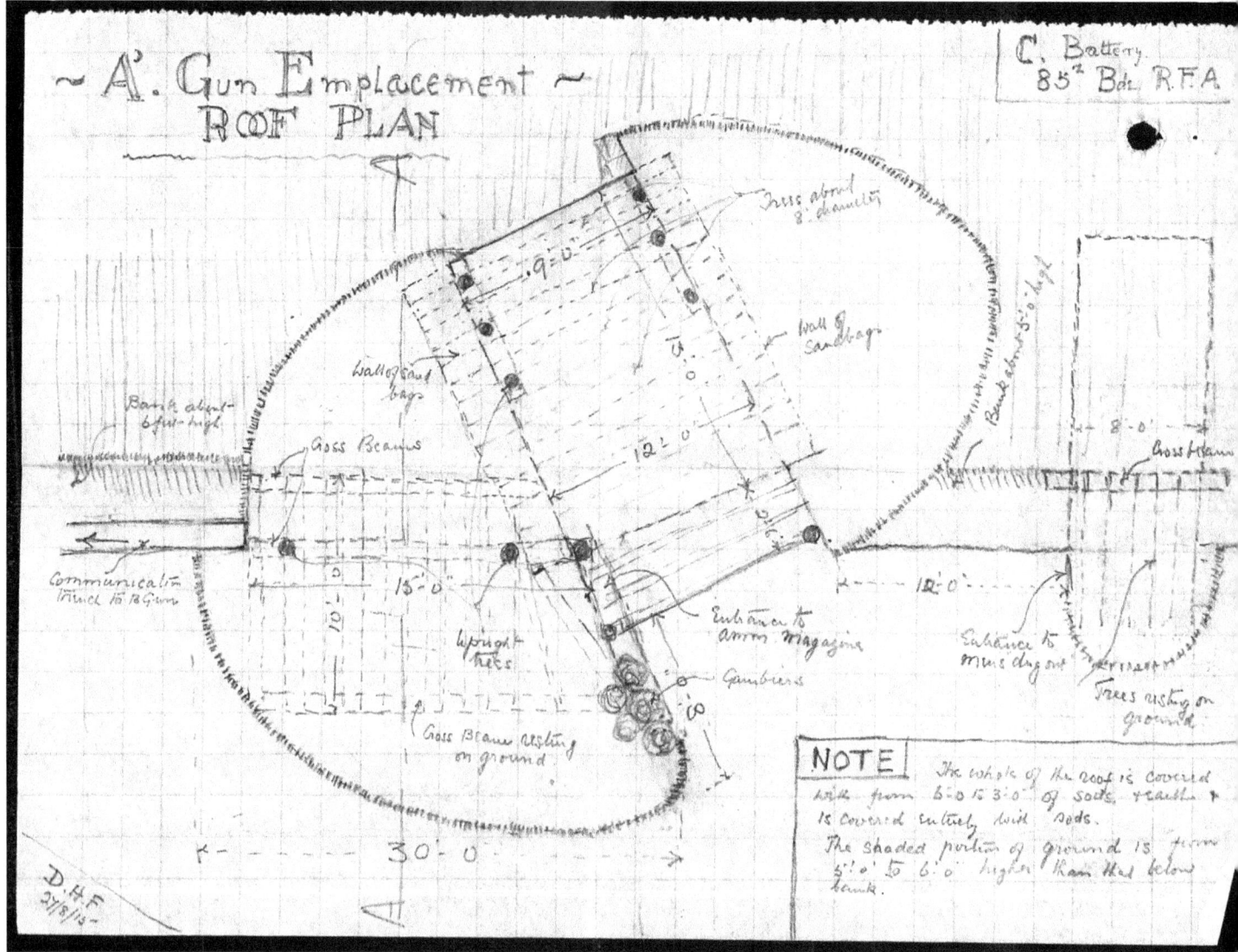

12/6607

18th Division

"D"/85 Battery R.F.A.
Vol. I

From 25th July to 31. Aug. 15.

WAR DIARY
or
INTELLIGENCE SUMMARY

(Erase heading not required.)

Army Form C. 2118

D Battery.

85th (How.) Bde R.F.A.

Officers Major James Carruthers. MVO D.S.O.
        Lieut L.I.C. PAUL
        Lieut R.W. GODFREY. (temp)
        2Lieut T.A JONES. (temp)

Strength 134 NCOs & Men
        125 Horses

Army Form C. 2118

WAR DIARY
or
INTELLIGENCE SUMMARY
(Erase heading not required.)

Instructions regarding War Diaries and Intelligence Summaries are contained in F.S. Regs., Part II. and the Staff Manual respectively. Title Pages will be prepared in manuscript.

Place	Date	Hour	Summary of Events and Information	Remarks and references to Appendices
Heytesbury	25/7/15	6 a.m.	Right Section moved off from camp under Lieuts Godfrey & Jones to entrain at Warminster for Southampton	
		7.15 a.m.	Left Section " " " " " " " " Lieut Paul	
Southampton	— " —		Guns and vehicles and horses embarked on S.S. Poetti, which steamed out from Southampton under torpedo destroyer escort at 4 p.m. Lieut Jones & 30 men crossed over on small paddle steamer "La Marguerite"	MCB
Havre	26/7/15	8 a.m.	Arrived at Quai & disembarked, & proceeded to Rest Camp No 5	MCB
	27/7/15	4.30 a.m.	The Battery moved off to Point 4, Gare des marchandises, where it entrained, under the direction of Major Carruthers R.T.O. "PP" Signal Section on same train. Arrived at detraining point near AMIENS at 5.30 p.m. and marched via AMIENS to VAUX-EN-AMIENOIS, where the 85 Brigade RFA was to be billeted. The gun park & horse lines were situated in an orchard.	MCB
VAUX	28/7/15	10.30 p.m.	Lieut PAUL proceeded with Brigade Major, 15 Div Art by motor to AVELUY, in the neighbourhood of which a battery position was reconnoitred. This part of the line was held by FRENCH troops and very quiet...... The Battery remained in billets.	MCB
	29/7/15	9.0 a.m.	The Battery marched out at 9 a.m. via ALLONVILLE – QUERRIEUX – to MERICOURT where it arrived at 3 p.m. and bivouacked in a meadow. The Battery from this day is attached to	MCB
MERICOURT L'ABBE			51st DIVISION (T.F.) and is attached to 1/3 HIGHLAND HOWITZER BDE R.F.A.	MCB
— " —	30/7/15		The battery remained in bivouac. MAJOR CARRUTHERS MVO DSO (Officer commanding) re-assumed command, having rejoined from special duty at HAVRE	MCB

WAR DIARY
or
INTELLIGENCE SUMMARY
(Erase heading not required.)

Army Form C. 2118

Instructions regarding War Diaries and Intelligence Summaries are contained in F. S. Regs., Part II. and the Staff Manual respectively. Title Pages will be prepared in manuscript.

Place	Date	Hour	Summary of Events and Information	Remarks and references to Appendices
MERICOURT	31/7/15		Major reconnoitred and decided on battery position near MARTINSART.	MB
M	1/8/15		The Officers, NCOs & Gunners proceeded mounted to battery position at MARTINSART to dig and prepare same. Horses and men back to MERICOURT	MB
MARTINSART	2/8/15		Guns and F.B. Wagons marched out from MERICOURT at 2 p.m. moving into position at 6 p.m. Horses and limbers returned to wagon line at MERICOURT	MB
MARTINSART	3/8/15		1 gun run out to a Forward Observing Station East of AVELUY. A/W Section registered several points in afternoon	MB
	4/8/15		Nos 2, 3 and 4 guns registered. Rained hard all day	MB
	5/8/15		Continued laying of telephone wires to trenches	MB
	6/8/15		Three HE shells fired from 77 mm. howitzer battery fell on right of battery position in afternoon.	MB
	7/8/15		Few enemy shells fired at MARTINSART. No 1 Gun registered. (F.O.O. in trenches)	MB
	8/8/15		The Wagon line moved to MOULIN des VIVIERS, S.E. of ALBERT. All guns fired a few rounds. No 4 fired at MILL near HAMEL (harbouring German snipers). Ranging by F.O.O. in trenches	MB

1875 Wt. W593/826 1,000,000 4/15 J.B.C. & A. A.D.S.S./Forms/C. 2118.

Army Form C. 2118

WAR DIARY
or
INTELLIGENCE SUMMARY
(Erase heading not required.)

Instructions regarding War Diaries and Intelligence Summaries are contained in F. S. Regs., Part II. and the Staff Manual respectively. Title Pages will be prepared in manuscript.

Place	Date	Hour	Summary of Events and Information	Remarks and references to Appendices
MARTINSART.	9/8/15		In morning No 4 again fired several rounds at MILL. Only slight damage done. General Stone (cmdg 18 Div Art.) & General McCarthy (cmdg 51st Div Art) visited the battery in morning	/4/
	10/8/15		Very heavy rain in evening.	/4/
	11/8/15		The Battery was visited by General Stone and Brigade Commander.	/4/
	12/8/15		A few rounds fired at Thiepval.	/4/
	13/8/15		Rain all day. No 2 Gun fired a few rounds at German trench mortar near CHATEAU THIEPVAL	/4/
	14/8/15		Slight rain. Quiet day.	/4/
	15/8/15		Quiet day. Fine.	/4/
	16/8/15		G.O.C. X Corps, G.O.C. R.A. X Corps & General McCarthy visited the battery. Fine. Re-registered several points after adjusting the sights. At 3:30 pm orders received from 18 Div. R.A. that battery was to be relieved that night by B/85 (cancelled). These orders were countermanded at 4:30 pm by G.O.C. X Corps, and the battery remained in position. Fine.	/4/
	17/8/15		Head Firing A/85 arrived in morning, being attached to instruction	/4/
	18/8/15		In afternoon fired several rounds at Trench Mortars at THIEPVAL. F.O.O failed to get telephone communication. Wet.	/4/
	19/8/15		In afternoon a short service was held by Padre. Fired 6 rounds at Trench Mortar at THIEPVAL. Molly fine. Head Firing returned to his battery	/4/

Army Form C. 2118

WAR DIARY
or
INTELLIGENCE SUMMARY

(Erase heading not required.)

Instructions regarding War Diaries and Intelligence Summaries are contained in F.S. Regs., Part II. and the Staff Manual respectively. Title Pages will be prepared in manuscript.

Place	Date	Hour	Summary of Events and Information	Remarks and references to Appendices
MARTINSART	20/8/15		A telephone line laid direct to trenches opposite THIEPVAL. Fine	AWP
	21/8/15		No 2 fired at trench mortar at 6pm. Appeared successful on the trench mortar battery (5 or 6 mortars) was silenced, and afterwards split up	AWP
	22/8/15		Fine day. Quiet.	AWP
	23/8/15		Fine. Few shells fired into MARTINSART (77mm gun)	AWP
	24/8/15		Fine. About 9pm fired two rounds in retaliation.	AWP
	25/8/15		Fine. Registered Point 417 (communication trench). Observing (F.O.O.) difficult owing to snipers from 424. 2 rounds at 424 silenced all sniping, allowing free observation of rounds on 417. Tried small Trytol shell most successful. In evening at 6pm fired 2 rounds at trench mortar at 384, with F.O.O.	AWP
	26/8/15		Fine day. Quiet. One round fired at 396 at 7pm in response to "TEST" call.	AWP
	27/8/15		Fired 13 rounds at Earthworks (Pt 408) with aid of F.O.O. Several direct hits which appeared to do little damage owing to solidity of the work. 2nd Lieut Fenton A/85 arrived for 3 days course of instruction	AWP
	29/8/15		A telephone wire was run out to left Sector to purpose of forward observing and intercommunication with trenches	AWP

Army Form C. 2118

WAR DIARY
or
INTELLIGENCE SUMMARY
(Erase heading not required.)

Instructions regarding War Diaries and Intelligence Summaries are contained in F. S. Regs., Part II. and the Staff Manual respectively. Title Pages will be prepared in manuscript.

Place	Date	Hour	Summary of Events and Information	Remarks and references to Appendices
MARTINSART	29/8/15		Fired a few rounds into redoubt at 40P, after 15 Siege Bty (6 inch howitzers) had severely knocked it about. Very wet evening and night.	
—	30/8/15		2nd Lieut Fenton A/85 left. Lieut Parker A/85 arrived for instruction	
—	31/8/15		In afternoon a few rounds were fired at a trench mortar located in trenches near CHATEAU THIEPVAL. Fine and cold.	

Maurice Ross-Major
O.C. B/85 RFA
31.8.15

85th Bde: A.C.
Vols: 1, 2, 3, 4, 5?

12/7910

18th Div.

CONFIDENTIAL

War Diary
of
85th B.A.C. R.F.A.

from

1st August – 31st August 1915

Vol I.

Aug 1915

CONFIDENTIAL

Army Form C. 2118.

Instructions regarding War Diaries and Intelligence Summaries are contained in F. S. Regs., Part II. and the Staff Manual respectively. Title pages will be prepared in manuscript.

WAR DIARY
or
INTELLIGENCE SUMMARY.
(Erase heading not required.)

85.² Howitzer Brigade
Ammunition Column R.F.A.
R.F.A.

Place	Date	Hour	Summary of Events and Information	Remarks and references to Appendices
			AUGUST 1915.	
(Ack-G)			Diary from July 25ᵗʰ – Aug 23ʳᵈ rendered by 85ᵗʰ Bgde H.Q.	
BONNAY	23.8.15	7/am	Arrived BONNAY. Lieut. B+D. Sutherland.	St. H.
	25.7.15	7.30	left BONNAY enroute TREUX, 9 Men Lieut B+D Sutherland.	St. H.
TREUX	28.7.15		Took over med iron letter from 83ʳᵈ Bgde R.F.A. at BUIRE, 21.3 G.S. Wagon 9 men, 15 L.D. Horses 100/100 S.A. Ammunition	St. L.
TREUX	31.8.15		Still at TREUX as 85 B+D Sutherland.	St. H.
			Officers of 85ᵗʰ Bgde. Amm. Col. R.F.A.	
			Lt. Houghton. Capt.	
			EB Sylvester 2ⁿᵈ Lt.	St. H.
			A.E. McPherson 2ⁿᵈ Lt. With D Sub at WARLOY.	
			Lt. Houghton Capt.	
			O.C. A/C 85ᵗʰ Bgde R.F.A.	

CONFIDENTIAL

War Diary
of
85TH B.A.C. R.F.A.
from
1st September to 30th September 1915

Vol 2.

CONFIDENTIAL.

Army Form C. 2118.

Instructions regarding War Diaries and Intelligence Summaries are contained in F. S. Regs., Part II. and the Staff Manual respectively. Title pages will be prepared in manuscript.

No. 2

WAR DIARY

OR

~~INTELLIGENCE SUMMARY~~

(Erase heading not required.)

81st Brigade.
Ammunition Col. R.F.A.

Place	Date	Hour	Summary of Events and Information	Remarks and references to Appendices
			SEPTEMBER 1915.	
TREUX	1.9.15		1st at TREUX. for B.A.D. Instruction.	App. A.
"	6.9.15		B. Section signed to wait from C. Battery.	App. B.
"			Commenced making up train for Vaudeuil. Drawing mules from ALBERT.	App. C
"	30.9.15		Left at TREUX. " D. " for instruction.	App D
			Officers, 2nd Lieut. Rev. Pet. R.F.A.	
			H. Hoyston. Capt.	
			E.C. Pelleter. 2nd Lt.	
			A. C. Stephens 2nd Lt. with D. Subsection at the VAUDRY.	App E.

H. Hoyston. Capt.
O.C. A/C. 81st Bde.
R.F.A.

Oct. 1915.

CONFIDENTIAL

War Diary
of
85th B.A.C. RFA

from

1st October – 31st October 1915

Vol 3

CONFIDENTIAL.

Army Form C. 2118.

WAR DIARY
or
INTELLIGENCE SUMMARY.

85th Brigade Ammn. Col. R.F.A.

Vol. 3

(Erase heading not required.)

Instructions regarding War Diaries and Intelligence Summaries are contained in F. S. Regs., Part II. and the Staff Manual respectively. Title pages will be prepared in manuscript.

Place	Date	Hour	Summary of Events and Information	Remarks and references to Appendices
TREUX	1.10.15		1st at TREUX Lieut D Robertson	Ap. A
	2.10.15		2nd Lt A.C. Stephen (in charge of D Section moving to Rest) was posted to us.	Ap. B
			Proceeded to 3rd Army French Cavalry School VALHEUREUX. Received horse dressings, concussion well, & troughs.	Ap. C Ap. D
	30.10.15		1st at TREUX Lieut D Robertson.	
			Officers of 85th Bde. Amm. Col. R.F.A.	Ap. E
			Lt. Haughton. Captn.
			E.C. Sylvester 2nd Lt.
			H. Haughton Captn.
			O.C. 85 Bde. Ammn Col. R.F.A.

CONFIDENTIAL

War Diary
of
85th B.A.C. R.F.A.
from
1st November — 30st November 1915

Vol 4.

CONFIDENTAL

Army Form C. 2118.

Vol. 4.

65th Bde
Ammunition Column R.F.A.

WAR DIARY
or
INTELLIGENCE SUMMARY.
(Erase heading not required.)

Place	Date	Hour	Summary of Events and Information	Remarks and references to Appendices
TREUX	1.11.15		NOVEMBER 1915. 1230 at Treux then D'Vischer.	P.H.
"	"		2nd Lt J.B. Parker posted to No 1 Column but attached to A Battery for duty.	K.O.
"	2.11.15		3 Ammunition (i. Shell) lorries available from D.A.C. or Park.	P.H. P.H.
"	30.11.15		Still at TREUX on D'Vischer.	P.H.
			Officers of est. 1/1 No 1 Pk H. Heysilver, Capt. E. O. Sylvester, 2nd Lt. J.B. Parker. 2nd Lt.	

H. Heysilver, Capt.
O.C. 1/c. 65th Bde R.F.A.

CONFIDENTIAL

War Diary
of
85th B.A.C. RFA.

from

1st December to 31st December

Vol. 5

CONFIDENTIAL.

Army Form C. 2118.

25th Howitzer
Ammunition Coln. 2 54

WAR DIARY
or
INTELLIGENCE SUMMARY.

(Erase heading not required.)

Instructions regarding War Diaries and Intelligence Summaries are contained in F. S. Regs., Part II. and the Staff Manual respectively. Title pages will be prepared in manuscript.

Place	Date	Hour	Summary of Events and Information	Remarks and references to Appendices
			DECEMBER 1915.	
TREUX	1.12.15		1Col at TREUX Sen. D. Labatie.	R.R.
"	26.12.15		B Ammunition Col.(Horse) 4 guns teams available	H.H.
"	31.12.15		1Col at TREUX Cen D Labatie	L.L.
			Officers of 25th Boh Amm. R.F.A.	
			Lt. Hagelin, Capt.	
			2nd Lt. Sylvester, 2nd Lieut.	H.L.
			J.B. Parker, 2nd Lieut (attached with Brigade)	
			Lt. Hagelin, Capt.	
			O.C. A/C 25th Bdn. R.F.A.	

T2134. Wt. W708—776. 500000. 4/15. Sir J. C. & S.

12/7051

18th Division

A/85 Battery. R.F.A.

Vol 3.

Sept. 15

WAR DIARY
or
INTELLIGENCE SUMMARY
(Erase heading not required.)

Army Form C. 2118

Instructions regarding War Diaries and Intelligence Summaries are contained in F.S. Regs., Part II. and the Staff Manual respectively. Title Pages will be prepared in manuscript.

Place	Date	Hour	Summary of Events and Information	Remarks and references to Appendices
BONNAY	1.9.15	—	Remained in billets	
VILLE SUR L'ANCRE	2.9.15	9.30 p.m.	Marched off 6.30 p.m. and into billets	
"	3.9.15	—	Remained in billets	
"	4.9.15	—	Morning Reconnoitred position near BÉCORDEL — BÉCOURT for one Section	
BÉCORDEL		4.30 p.m.	Commenced digging in Right Section	
"	5.9.15		Work continued Right Section	
"	6.9.15		Reconnoitred position for Left Section in woods S.W. of BÉCOURT	
"	7.9.15	8 p.m.	Left Section came into action	
"	8.9.15	7 p.m.	Right Section came into action	
"	9.9.15		Work continued on Emplacements. Registration of targets on to hour carried out for Left Section but it was not possible — Ditto —	
"	10.9.15			
"	11.9.15	3.30 p.m.	Commenced registration of points in enemy's trenches with Left Section. Amm" Expended 15 BX	
"	12.9.15	2.30 a.m.	" " " " — Right Section } Amm" Expended 11 BX 6 B.	
"			Continued " " " — Left Section	
"	13.9.15		Work continued on Emplacements. Storage 1. C. I. D. evacuated sick	
"	14.9.15 to 17.9.15		Work continued on Emplacements	
"	18.9.15		Received orders to move Left Section to new position near ALBERT. In forenoon Reconnoitred position N.E. of ALBERT on outskirts of the town. Afternoon brought up ammunition to Left Section and sent off to prepare hut at VILLE	

WAR DIARY
or
INTELLIGENCE SUMMARY
(Erase heading not required.)

Army Form C. 2118

Place	Date	Hour	Summary of Events and Information	Remarks and references to Appendices
ALBERT BECORDEL	19.9.15	5 a.m.	Left Section came out of action and moved to ALBERT	
	20.9.15		Afternoon B.C. Staff moved to ALBERT Reconnoitred observation stations	
			Right Section moved from VILLE SUR L'ANCRE to S.W. of ALBERT.	
	21.9.15		Left Section worked on emplacements	
			Right Section continued registration. Amm" Expended 20 Bx 3 B. Stores 1 LD howr toener (sick)	
ALBERT	23.9.15	11 a.m.	Afternoon and evening A Subsection gun and amm" moved to new position at ALBERT	
		12.30 pm	Received orders to bring Left Section into action	
		2.14 pm	Left Section occupied prepared position	
		8.45 pm	Commenced registering points in enemy's trenches. Amm" expended 37 Bx	
			Retaliated (2 Rounds Bx) on LA-BOISELLE to trench mortar fire	
ALBERT	24.9.15	2 pm	Continued registration with Left Section and A Sub Amm" 3.5" Bx	
		10.5 pm	Retaliated on LA-BOISELLE for trench mortar fire Amm" 4 Bx	
			Enemy 1 R1 Howr. fired 5 rounds.	
			Retaliated on LA-BOISELLE for trench mortar fire. Amm" 4 Bx	
	25.9.15	6 am	Bombarded LA BOISELLE and taken part of German trenches to Eastward	
		2 pm to 5 pm	Amm" Expended 85' Bx S'B.	
		2 pm	Remaining gun of Right Section came into action at ALBERT having been moved from BECORDEL in the morning	
	26.9.15		Continued registration	
			Retaliated to trench mortars during the night	

Army Form C. 2118

WAR DIARY
or
INTELLIGENCE SUMMARY
(Erase heading not required.)

Instructions regarding War Diaries and Intelligence Summaries are contained in F. S. Regs., Part II. and the Staff Manual respectively. Title Pages will be prepared in manuscript.

Place	Date	Hour	Summary of Events and Information	Remarks and references to Appendices
ALBERT	27.9.15		During afternoon retaliated to enemy mortar fire and again at night. Shrapnel 1 gunner found from Base Havre.	
"	28.9.15		Morning, afternoon sniper retaliated to enemy mortar in LA BOISELLE.	
"	29.9.15 9.30 a.m.		One enemy shell (110 mm) fell in brigade lines — no damage or casualties. Evening retaliated to enemy mortar fire.	
"	30.9.15		A morning, evening, and at night retaliates to enemy mortar fire.	

A. Shuttleworth Major R.A.
Comdg. A/R.A. Idea R.F.A.

B/85 Barry
fols: 3, 4, 5.

121/7795

18th Kurrein

Sept. 15 Oct & Nov.

CONFIDENTIAL

WAR DIARY

OF

'B' BATTERY 85TH BDE R.F.A.

FROM 1ST SEPTEMBER TO 30TH SEPT 1915

(VOLUME III).

WAR DIARY or INTELLIGENCE SUMMARY

B Batty. 85th Bde R.F.A.

Army Form C. 2118

(Erase heading not required.)

Place	Date	Hour	Summary of Events and Information	Remarks and references to Appendices
BRAY SUR-SOMME	1/IX	—	Construction of Gunpits continued. Men were employed in shifts and good progress was made. Relief of men were frequently brought from the wagon line at VILLE-SUR-L'ANCRE. The soil was a clayey nature with chalk and flint subsoil. The weather was favourable, very little rain being experienced.	S31
	6-7/IX night of		One of left section were brought up from wagon line at VILLE-SUR-L'ANCRE and placed in pits.	S32
	7/IX		Left section commenced registration of targets.	S33
	7/8/IX night of		Guns of right section were brought up from VILLE-SUR-L'ANCRE and placed into pits.	S33
	8/IX		Right section commenced registration of targets.	
			Whilst the digging of the gun pits was proceeding the battery staff were engaged in laying wire to F.O.O. positions, the general idea being to have a loop wire running in the forward trenches into which the observing officers could tap, the ends being brought back to the battery operator. Difficulty was experienced owing to the poor quality and lack of uniformity of the wire supplied.	S34

Army Form C. 2118

WAR DIARY

~~INTELLIGENCE SUMMARY~~

'B' Batty 85th Bde R.F.A.

(Erase heading not required.)

Instructions regarding War Diaries and Intelligence Summaries are contained in F.S. Regs., Part II. and the Staff Manual respectively. Title Pages will be prepared in manuscript.

Place	Date	Hour	Summary of Events and Information	Remarks and references to Appendices
VILLE-SUR-L'ANCRE TO MEAULTE.	18/IV	7.30 pm	The wagon line was moved from the MAIRIE of VILLE-SUR-L'ANCRE to billets at South end of the village of MEAULTE - (Café du Broc). Water for animals was obtained from the ANCRE stream and water for men from local wells.	JM
BRAY.	21/IV	9.15 am	Several H.E. shells burst on the slope behind the gun pits and one gunner was wounded in the leg & thigh with fragments of shell. This was the first casualty in the battery caused by enemy fire.	SM
"			The remainder of the month was occupied with the negotiation of dugouts, the completion of the gun pits, and the ordinary fatigues of the camp.	SM

CONFIDENTIAL

WAR DIARY

OF

'B' BATTERY 85TH BDE R.F.A

FROM 1ST OCTOBER TO 31ST OCT 1915

(VOLUME IV).

Army Form C. 2118

WAR DIARY
or
INTELLIGENCE SUMMARY 'B' Batty 85th Bde. R.F.A.

(Erase heading not required.)

Instructions regarding War Diaries and Intelligence Summaries are contained in F.S. Regs., Part II. and the Staff Manual respectively. Title Pages will be prepared in manuscript.

Place	Date	Hour	Summary of Events and Information	Remarks and references to Appendices
FRANCE. BRAY SUR SOMME	1/X		Work was continued on gun pits. Fatigue parties were engaged on building some quarters for the officers and men of the gun position. Work was also done on a telephone dugout near No 4 gun pit and connected by a passage to the gun pit. Wires were laid to the other pits. The battery staff were employed in the maintenance and laying of wires and operating.	SJW
"	26/X	3.30pm	A gunner of the battery staff was slightly wounded in the hand by shrapnel whilst working on a wire.	JW
MEAULTE.	1/X		The men at the wagon line were engaged in rebuilding stable buildings, water troughs etc. beside the ordinary work of grooming and exercising horses.	SW
			During the month the weather generally was fine, and good progress was made in the work of providing winter quarters.	

1875 Wt. W593/826 1,000,000 4/15 J.B.C. & A. A.D.S.S./Forms/C. 2118.

CONFIDENTIAL.

WAR DIARY
OF
'B' BATTERY 85TH BDE R.F.A.

FROM 1ST NOVEMBER TO 30TH NOV 1915.

(VOLUME V).

Army Form C. 2118

WAR DIARY
or
~~INTELLIGENCE SUMMARY~~

'B' Batty 85th Bde
R.F.A.

(Erase heading not required.)

Instructions regarding War Diaries and Intelligence Summaries are contained in F.S. Regs., Part II. and the Staff Manual respectively. Title Pages will be prepared in manuscript.

Place	Date	Hour	Summary of Events and Information	Remarks and references to Appendices
FRANCE PRAY SUR SOMME	1/VI		The battery remained in action - in the same gun pits - Usual targets were registered and ordinary work carried on. Fatigue parties were employed in lagging the passages leading to the gunpits and in building winter quarters as well as the ordinary fatigues of the camp. The weather was generally fine but cold. Rain was experienced and towards the end of the month light falls of snow.	J.N.
MEAULTE	1/VII		Besides the ordinary work of securing horses and supplying the gun positions, fatigue parties were employed in constructing new stable accommodation and the repair of the previously existing buildings. Such footways and roads were formed.	S.N.

J.N. Skelton

12/7051

18th Division

C/85 Battery
Vol 2
Sept 15

To AG 3rd Echelon

Herewith the War Diary of
C/85 R.I.A. for the month of
September.

3.10.45

W. Hurriston ?
Capt
Cmdg C/85

1.9.15. Combined shoot arranged for 3 pm with Q.R.H.A. & C/82 to shell Hidden Wood at pt 303. Heavy rain & bad telephones caused it to be a failure. 6 rnds HE fired.

2.9.15. Fired 5 rds HE at rifle grenade battery near pt 486 at 4 am — Last round reported to have set alight something just behind tgt.
Also registered trench from pt 784 to pt 478 — This was to be used in case of an attack on the Division on our left.

3.9.15. Engaged catapult bomb thrower near pt 985.

7.9.15
8.9.15   Registered the front trench from pt 301 to the left to the craters. Also triangle of trenches near Pt 4.6.15. This was in preparation for a projected attack on this piece of trench.
Registering difficult owing to variety of ammunition — Cordite of various lots & Ballistite — Long HE & Short HE shell — Lyddite, TNT, trotyl of several marks. The weights of shell varying in some cases over 1 lb from average.

12.9.15. Shoot arranged for 3.30 pm to destroy enemy's breastworks in new mine crater near Point 301. Trenches 77, 98, 79 cleared — at 3.30 pm Q.R.H.fired 14 rounds followed by C/85 with 14 HE followed by C/84 — 18/pdr.
Flank observations sent from Kirsch Trench by Lt Ricketts. B.C. at battery observation posts & reports sent back from front trench by F.O.O. of C/84. Four rounds observed to drop into the crater, 4 others to strike the lip of the crater.
Flank observation from L 33-1.5-1.5
Battery   "   P 14 - 6 - 9
Battery position "   P 8. 1 - 0
F.O.O.   "   P 10 7 - 7

17.9.15. Arranged with O.C. R.Fusiliers to have a portion of trenches 80 & 81 cleared & shelled "the sniper's den" in the right hand of two craters near BOIS ALLEMAND. Very successful Lt Ricketts F.O.O. Wire blown away parapet damaged & 1 German blown onto the parapet.

19.9.15. Took over fresh zone that is to cover sectors D_3 & E_1 instead of $D_1 D_2 D_3$. This is due to rearrangement of infantry; three groups of artillery formed. The Wagon line shifted back to DERNANCOURT to make way for the Right Group wagon lines. Observation of trenches North of 477 only to be carried out from NE corner of BECOURT WOOD. Emplacements slightly altered to obtain $5°$ m L. Total now about $70°$ of front.
Registration of E1 carried out.

23.9.15. General bombardment from 2 pm Targets in D_3 sector, not rehearsal but registration 47 rds Ballistite shooting map range Cordite requiring 150 yds more at 3000.

24.9.15 Similar to 23rd but with different tasks. 53 rounds

25.9.15 Similar to 24th but time was 2-4 pm, then pause till 4.45, when rapid bombardment till 5pm. Front narrowed down to 479-483. The Germans did not reply to the bombardment except a

C/85 Railway R7a.
Vol: 3/2-3

121/7936

SENT

18th K m

WAR DIARY or INTELLIGENCE SUMMARY

Army Form C. 2118

C/85 RHA Batteries September 1915 Meuwelk[?]

Place	Date	Hour	Summary of Events and Information	Remarks and references to Appendices
Meuwelk	1.9.15		Combined shoot arranged for 3pm with Q. RHA & Y/82 RFA to shell Hidden Wood at pt 303 – Heavy rain & bad telephones caused it to be a failure. 6 rds HE fired.	
	2.9.15		Fired 5 rds HE at rifle grenade battery near pt 486 at 4 am – Last round reported to have set alight something behind the target – Also registered trench from pt 784 to pt 476 – This trench to be shelled in case of an attack by the Division on our left.	
	3.9.15		Engaged catapult bomb thrower near pt 485	
	7.9.15		Registered the front line from pt 301 to the left of the crater. Also tried trench mortar near pt 615 – This was in preparation for our projected attack on this piece of trench –	
			Registration difficult owing to variety of ammunition. Engaged various lots of Ballistite – low HE, & short HE shell – lyddite, TNT, &c – The weights of shell varying in some cases by 1 lb from average.	
	12.9.15		Shoot arranged for 3.30pm to destroy enemy breastwork in new mine crater near pt 30 – Trenches 77,18,19 cleared at 3.30pm – Q RHA fired 14 rds followed by C/85 with 14 HE followed by Y/84. 18 fsm – Flank observation sent in from	

WAR DIARY or INTELLIGENCE SUMMARY

Army Form C. 2118

C/85 R.F.A. October ~~September~~ 1915

Minimising ~~CahN~~

Place	Date	Hour	Summary of Events and Information	Remarks and references to Appendices
	17.9.15		from Kirsch Trench by Lt Ricketts R.C. at battery observation post & reports sent back from front trench by F.O.O. of C/64. — Form rounds appears to drop into the crater, & others to strike the lip of the crater, — Flash observation from L.33.15.15. Bty observation from P.14.69. Bty position P.8 — 1.0 — F.O.O. P.10 — 7.7. Arranged with O.C. R. Fusiliers to have a portion of trenches 80 N & I cleared & shelled "the sniper's den" in the right hand of the two craters near BOIS ALLEMAND. very successful — It Ricketts F.O.O. line blown away/parapet damaged/ German flare fired outside parapet — Took over fresh gun, that is to cover sectors D3 & E, instead of D, D2, D3. This is due to rearrangement of infantry; three groups of Artillery running. The wagon line shifted back to DERNANCOURT to make way for the R.H.F. group wagon lines. Observation of trenches N of PT. 87.17 only to be carried on from N.E. Corner of BÉCOURT WOOD. E. emplacement slightly altered to allow 5m.L. total more about 70° of front. Registration of F1 carried out.	
	18.9.15			

WAR DIARY
or
INTELLIGENCE SUMMARY

Army Form C. 2118

(Erase heading not required.)

SSGA September 1915

Place	Date	Hour	Summary of Events and Information	Remarks and references to Appendices
Meault	23.9.15		General bombardment from 2pm - Targets in D 3 sector, not rehearsed but registration - 47 rnds - Ballistic shooting map range - Corrosite regiment 150 more at 3.000 - Similar to 23rd but with different tasks 53 rounds -	
	24.9.15			
	25.9.15		Similar to 24th but time was 2-4pm then paused till 5pm. Front narrowed down to 479-483. The Germans did not reply to the bombardment except a few rounds on the TAMBOUR & some on the 18pr bty. News received that the advance both has been at front 18per bty. News received that the advance extended today 66 to 18 X proper made. Ammunition expended today	
24 AP 25 - 26 23rd			Heavy rain most of both days. 14 Allies aeroplanes went over Eastwards at about 6am through heavy artillery fire; only one had to return at this period - 12 rounds of HE fired at 5.30am as programme here for the infantry to simulate an attack should the Germans have parapets & there suffer loss from such - Very rainy morning. Effect not noticeable - Machine gun emplacements were shelled but orders were received that no artillery ammunition was to be expended except at the call of the infantry - News of the	
26.9.15				
26.9.15 30.9.15				

WAR DIARY October 1915

INTELLIGENCE SUMMARY

Army Form C. 2118

Place	Date	Hour	Summary of Events and Information	Remarks and references to Appendices
Meuville	29.9.15		of the progress of the advance was sent through daily from H.Q. All preparations were made for the artillery bombardment preliminary to an attack.	
	29&30		Weather improves but distinctly colder — our observation station shelled 15 & 12 lbs from 4.2 howitzer.	

WAR DIARY or INTELLIGENCE SUMMARY

Army Form C. 2118

C/185 R.F.A. October

Place	Date	Hour	Summary of Events and Information	Remarks and references to Appendices
	3/10/15		Ammunition very sparingly allotted, and only for Special Calls from Infantry. 11 rounds fired at a supposed emplacement at the 4'of Pont 48.5, and a direct hit on the point was obtained. Observation from the TAMBOUR. Col: English present.	
	6/10/15		The Infantry (E. Surreys) Reported a machine gun in the Centre of the Loyonge Wood — N° 3 gun fired 8 rounds - Amatol - It appears to require 100 yards more range than T.N.T. Again called upon to retaliate on trenches opposite the Tambour - 4 Rounds H.E.	
	9/10/15		The Intermediate and 2nd Line positions were reconnoitred, the gun positions and observation stations selected.	
	10/10/15		Allotment for the week 40 Shrapnel, No H.E. The Germans have begun firing large trench mortars East into Tambour, after a few days into De Lisle's near station. At least 4 different mortars have been located. One was shelled with the Shrapnel. A few very good rounds were obtained, of which the bullets splashed the mortars position, but as the mortar continued firing, they are probably fired from under overhead cover.	
	13/10/15		The "Wagon line" was shifted from DERNANCOURT to RIBEMONT on account of an outbreak of a form of neurosis, cracked heels caused by the highly manured soil, and the wet condition of the field in which they were put; a but brick standings. The disease starts with a few small boils round the fetlock of horses. When the horse is removed and groomed, the skin around the boil appears inflamed under the hair and in a few days the boil bursts and the skin for an inch or two round it comes off leaving a raw place, which if left in the cribs, the horse falls dead. But buists. Course of cure varies from 5 days to a fortnight, at-	

WAR DIARY or INTELLIGENCE SUMMARY

Army Form C. 2118

185 RFA October Confidential Copy

Place	Date	Hour	Summary of Events and Information	Remarks and references to Appendices
	15/10/15		The present positions of the Wagon lines at Ribemont (6 mils) and the gun line and intermediate positions 1½ miles from guns. No HE shell being allotted.	
	18th to 23rd/10/15		During the past week only 32 rounds of shrapnel. Owing to the success Germans making the trenches and dugouts near the observing Station into redoubts, the Station has had its scrutiny on the 16th, 17th & 18th. The Battery has had occasional pairs of rounds fired into it, but no damage has been done, though the line is cut and both phone and mines rounds have been had. Only Shrapnel was allotted but at especial gains of O.C. & Siryes as a German mine had been blown up on the Tambour and Casualties were being caused by the Mortars - 6 replacements all used by trench mortars were located & registered.	
	23/10/15		Work on the 2nd line positions commenced. The intermediate positions prepared with the exception of revetting the sides of the shelters fired which is in Crumbling chalk. Ensted ammunition supply.	
	25/9/15		D.H.Q. R.A. to send orderly from HEILLY to Ribemont. Message left by cyclist orderly 8.30pm also via telephone to arrived at Battery 10.30pm. Telephone message arrived 9.34. 2nd wagon left 9.27. Wagon left 9.36 at Battery 11.3pm. The 2nd wagon had not been warned for duty 9.34 arrived. Should have arrived half an hour sooner. The telephone message Ribemont is just over 6 miles from Battery. The weather was very bad, raining hard. Three observation balloons being up made shooting inadvisable.	
	27/10/15 28/10/15		Lt. Ricketts suggested the four guns only X, Y & Z. This will enable us to search the whole of the front trench opposite E Sector as the line of fire enfilades the German trenches	

Wt. W593/826 1,000,000 4/15 J.B.C. & A. A.D.S.S./Forms/C.2118.

Army Form C. 2118

C/85 RFA November 1915
W. Hunter Capt.

WAR DIARY
or
INTELLIGENCE SUMMARY
(Erase heading not required.)

Instructions regarding War Diaries and Intelligence Summaries are contained in F.S. Regs., Part II. and the Staff Manual respectively. Title Pages will be prepared in manuscript.

Place	Date	Hour	Summary of Events and Information	Remarks and references to Appendices
	31/10/15		16 Shrapnel & 4 HE fired at various targets to check registration. — Allotment for week ending 31/10 = 26 Shrapnel, 34 HE. Only 24 and 30 fired. The alternative position nearly completed. The intermediate position finished metal material is available for roofing	
	1/11/15		The 2nd line position — digging at A gun Completed & B gun commenced. Wagon line to remain at ABBE MBWT	
	2/11/15		Allotment - 34 B X 6 Shrapnel	
	3rd 4th		Fired — 26 " " "	
	3rd	4pm	Selived Germans who were throwing bombs & grenades into Tambour by 4 4 2 rounds BX. Selived an A.A. gun which had been pushed up to the Eastern outskirts of FRICOURT. Remainder of week very quiet owing to fog.	
	4/15 5/11/15		4/ rounds fired at Lozenge Wood & 4 at Abri Wood. Fired during week 26 BX — owing to call from E Surreys holding TAMBOUR, fired 10 rounds at trench opposite N.9 F3 e 5½" by J faus steel on the parapet on into the trench.	
			During week officers Cookhouse Completed. Magazines nearly Completed, to enable our wagon load after gun to be stowed away from bomb pits or dug outs	
	6/11/15 7/11/15		No Casualties. Chipped first post with Cox axe felling timber.	

WAR DIARY
INTELLIGENCE SUMMARY November 1915

Army Form C. 2118

W Shinnton Capt

Place	Date	Hour	Summary of Events and Information	Remarks and references to Appendices
	8/11/15		We again fired at the trenches opposite the Tambour, as established for silence by Commander; 11.19X, & in the afternoon 5 BX to silence mortars, this finished the weeks allotment of 36 BX leaving 6 B. of which 4 were expended on the 11th at 5 p.m. on a cammouflet being fired by us at the TAMBOUR. — 2 more on Sunday 14th for registration.	
	14/11/15		The B.C. went up on an aeroplane reconnaissance over the line near FRICOURT, MAMETZ and registered the A BR1 Wood dug-outs which appears to be the H.Q. of a Battalion — firing 6s the signals from the Wireless having to be transmitted by telephone through an exchange. Communication was not satisfactory. 6 Gas BX were fired. The Battery's position and the alternative position are not mutually conspicuous. New officers dug out completed, also magazines for each section to accommodate 48 rounds per gun in boxes. Improved Cookhouse commenced.	
	23/11/15		During past week we have fired allotment of 46 BX of this 16 were fired from the alternative position by D Gun, which shot very well — 12 targets were registered in spite of a numbered shoot. Point '61' in E Sector was shelled — The demolition for Cord'te is now about 10% of the range temperature being about 35 average. J "C"Gun pit — not having sufficient corrugated iron supplied also Cookhouse.	
	30/11/15		During past week we have fired 53 BX, out of allotment of 50. The new officers mess was leaked, and has been rebuilt; it is now much stronger and drier. Some new shell fuses near Point 77 were registered; otherwise ammunition was chiefly expended in	

WAR DIARY or INTELLIGENCE SUMMARY

C/85 RFA December

Place	Date	Hour	Summary of Events and Information	Remarks and references to Appendices
Meaulte	25/12/15		On 25th 18 bombs were dropped on MERICOURT by German Aeroplanes in retaliation for air raid by us. Several men & horses killed & wounded. Part of B/85 wagon line only had narrow escapes. D Subsection dug out and making merriest. 26th 9-6.30 am 10 off quiet. The weather has been much colder, on a living room and making merriest. 29th 9-6.30 am 10 off quiet. The correction to map range for Cordite now being nearly 400 at H = 4000. Ballistics only very slightly affected.	
	26/12/15		3rd Army Survey Section attached themselves for pay & rations from 24th. New Emplacements for 2nd line position dug by Tunnelling Company at D29a27. owing to misunderstanding by O.C. Brigade. The partially completed ones dug by us to be retained as alternative positions — Capt. Lieut. Starns, 2 Sergts 6 Telephonists, 2nd Glamorgan Howitzer Battery 53 Div Arty. Welsh Territorials attached for 10 days instruction.	
	27/12/15		12 Rounds Bx fired at F.3.c 6.9m connection with springing of a mine at F.3.c.5.8. Allotment for week 50 Bx all expended — Weather very mild, and with the incessant dripping trench without revetting has made trench to O.P. impassable. Orders received to get alternative position ready for occupation at once —	

WAR DIARY or INTELLIGENCE SUMMARY

Army Form C. 2118

C/1/5 RFA   December

Place: Meaulte Camp

Date	Hour	Summary of Events and Information	Remarks and references to Appendices
5/12/15 to 12/12/15		Wet weather causing the Trenches everywhere to fall in. The Trench to the observation station impassable. The Pioneers being began for the forward trenches. Allotment 83° OX – 84 Fred; at M.G. emplacements in the front line and some distant points for registration. A 2nd Battery from the 2nd Glamorgan Battery T.F. attached for instruction. The alternative position handed over to left Group. The German gun here appears to have suffered as their working parties had to work on the top.	
13/12/15 to 17/12/15		Weather much drier. Leaking dug outs repaired, more wire trenches dug. Allotment 80 OX. All expended mostly retaliation. Station shelling blowing up the dug out. An advanced position at F3 a 9.0 for one Howitzer at 1458b for barbed and wire run out on 16/12/15 – but awaiting order to mount gun. To cut wire at point X 20 b 8.1.	
18/12/15		1st Welsh Battery (Glamorgan) 53 Div Arty arrived to occupy our alternative position. Lt Irish showed them in. Amn 18 pr Battery also came up by an alternative position – and are both under Turnour Battle on an extra Group or the same zone.	

WAR DIARY December

INTELLIGENCE SUMMARY Mametz Camp

Army Form C. 2118

Place	Date	Hour	Summary of Events and Information	Remarks and references to Appendices
	26/12/15		On the 24th the Glamorgan Battery was withdrawn after registering on 3 days. On night of 24th-25th the Germans shelled the TAMBOUR heavily with shells and bombs until 11·15 pm. 6/85 fired 22 in retaliation — allotment so named to 55. Expended 88 18X + 15"B including 20 18X + 15"B fired on 26th at 11.33 am, 12.33 pm + 2.35 pm in connection with a bombardment of the S.W. Corner of FRICOURT. by 9", 6", 4.1", 60 prs Field Artillery. The houses and trenches were knocked about, but no movement of Germans was seen. The men had excellent meals on Xmas day — made up by presents and a grant of 10/- from Battery funds. Seeing they are quite cut off and upon Xmas day.	

Army Form C. 2118

WAR DIARY or INTELLIGENCE SUMMARY

Y/55 RFA December

(Erase heading not required.)

Place	Date	Hour	Summary of Events and Information	Remarks and references to Appendices
Meaulte	28th		A mine was sprung by us at F.3.c.5.9 at 3.30 p.m. — after a pause of 25 minutes the infantry gave the signal for concentrated fire — trenches opposite the TAMBOUR — Y/55 fired 28 x 15 BX — after 20 minutes firing, the infantry started digging a new trench along the lips of the craters —	
	29th		Allotment from Sunday to Wednesday 24 noon — 13B, 45 BX all expended — at about 12.45 p.m. the Germans started shelling the TAMBOUR and Dr Wilall nature of fire & howitzer up to 8" howitzer — Y/85 retaliated with 53 rds BX on 20 K spots all round the TAMBOUR & at FRICOURT FM M. by 4.30 pm the heaviest fire was reached & they shelled with "tear" shell also a few at the battery — at 5.30 pm all guns were down — The Germans having succeeded in cutting out a party of 20 men in a sap out —	
	30th		Another move similar to 28th Y/55 fired 28 20 BT Allotment till Wed nearly for week 160 BX & 30 B to include	
	31st		indenting ammunition — Weather slightly misor —	

W Humphreys Capt
RFA
Cmdg Y/55

121/6971

18th Division

2/85 Battery RFA.
Vol: II

Sep 1. 15

WAR DIARY
or
INTELLIGENCE SUMMARY

(Erase heading not required.)

Army Form C. 2118

Instructions regarding War Diaries and Intelligence Summaries are contained in F.S. Regs., Part II. and the Staff Manual respectively. Title Pages will be prepared in manuscript.

Place	Date	Hour	Summary of Events and Information	Remarks and references to Appendices
MARTINSART	1.9.15		No firing to-day. Wet.	Reference to PLAN DIRECTEUR 2 BIS
	2.9.15		A few shells were fired into MARTINSART from a battery N.E. of THIEPVAL. Lieut Parker A/85 rejoined his battery. Wet.	
	3.9.15		Fired 3 rounds in morning at 40S. (Earthworks)	M.R
	4.9.15		Fired 3 rounds at 40S in conjunction with 15th Siege Bty RGA (6in How). Effect very good. In afternoon again in conjunction with 15th Siege fired 8 rounds on a large working party digging a trench W. of POZIERES. Battery work ceased. A fine day. 4 Shells fired into MARTINSART at 11 a.m.	M.R
	5.9.15		At midday fired 9 rounds at working party near POZIERES causing work to cease. Fine day.	M.R
	6.9.15		A fine day. At 9.40 pm fired 19 rounds at 40S at request of Infantry, who were suffering from Trench Mortar opposite that point.	M.R
	7.9.15		In afternoon fired 3 rounds at 40S and 3 into THIEPVAL. At 8.30 pm fired 6 trench mortar near 39T at request of Infantry. Fine.	M.R
	8.9.15		At 4.40 pm 4 shells were fired into MARTINSART. In retaliation we fired 3 into POZIERES in conjunction with "X" Bty R.H.A. Fine.	M.R
	9.9.15		At 7.15 pm fired one round at Trench mortar at 39S, which did not reply. Very fine day.	M.R
	10.9.15		At 3 pm fired 17 rounds at earth works ab. 40S and again 8 shells at 11 pm with good effect. The rounds fired at 11pm were in conjunction with the Batteries 5/the R.H.A., in response to a message from the Infantry that the Germans were mending the wire which had been damaged earlier in the day by Howitzer fire.	M.R

Army Form C. 2118

WAR DIARY
or
INTELLIGENCE SUMMARY
(Erase heading not required.)

Instructions regarding War Diaries and Intelligence Summaries are contained in F. S. Regs., Part II. and the Staff Manual respectively. Title Pages will be prepared in manuscript.

Place	Date	Hour	Summary of Events and Information	Remarks and references to Appendices
MARTINSART	11.9.15	At 3pm	fired 15 rounds at trenches round 398 where Trench Mortar was reported to be. Several direct hits on the trenches were obtained. A tree OP was chosen in BOIS D'AVELUY and a rope ladder erected. Fine	MGP
	12.9.15	At 6.15 am	a TEST CONCENTRATION was ordered. At 8.30 pm at request of infantry 2 rounds were fired at trench mortar at 396. Kent Paul went to England today on leave. Fine	MGP
	13.9.15		In evening fired 2 rounds at trench Mortar at point 396. Fine	MGP
	14.9.15	3.15pm	Fired 6 rounds at Point 398, securing two direct hits in trench	MGP
		3.30pm	5 " " 383	
		5.15pm	" 14 " Artillery O P at Pt 5537 G 26. After shooting at the O P the Guns were relaid on MESNIL with a Howitzer. Fine	MGP
	14.9.15	At 7.15 pm	fired 40 rounds at points 398 - 394 by order of GOC G Sector	MGP
	15.9.15	At 11.45 am	fired 3 rounds at point 398. Fine	MGP
	16.9.15		Fired 3 rounds at 398 in morning	MGP
	17.9.15		Fine. Quiet day	MGP
	18.9.15	4pm	Fired 14 rounds at 401 & trenches round CHATEAU THIEPVAL	MGP
		6.30pm	16 " " trenches at 408 in reply to hostile bombardment of our trenches opposite that point	MGP

Army Form C. 2118

WAR DIARY
or
INTELLIGENCE SUMMARY
(Erase heading not required.)

Instructions regarding War Diaries and Intelligence Summaries are contained in F. S. Regs., Part II. and the Staff Manual respectively. Title Pages will be prepared in manuscript.

Place	Date	Hour	Summary of Events and Information	Remarks and references to Appendices
MARTINSART	19.9.15	4.30pm	Fired 16 rounds at Point 408. Fine	MSB
	20.9.15		Fine. Quiet	MSB
	21.9.15		Fired one round at 1.30 p.m. in retaliation to Trench Mortar at 408. Trench howr. attacked to 7th right. Instruction from 34th Division.	MSB
	22.9.15	10.15am	Fired one round at 408 ⎫	MSB
		12.30	" " " " ⎬ at request of Infantry
		3.30 pm	11 " at 398 ⎪
			6 " " 396 ⎭
		10 pm	West Paul returned from leave	
	27.9.15		At 8 a.m. 14 French VOISIN aeroplanes flew over on way to raid VALENCIENNES. At 1pm registered Church at POZIERES. At 3pm commenced bombardment of 408-411 getting a hit direct hits on what appeared to be Machine gun emplacements. 50 rounds were fired. At 4pm fired at 396 (2 rounds) in reply to Trench Mortar fire.	MSB
	28.9.15		At 2 pm fired 40 rounds at bok trenches at 404. At 2.20 pm fired 10 rounds at Tower NW 6) THIEPVAL. Wet	MSB
	29.9.15		Wet Slow bombardment of trenches by no 5 till 4pm from 4 pm to 5pm intense bombardment. 100 rounds were fired.	MSB

Army Form C. 21

WAR DIARY
or
INTELLIGENCE SUMMARY
(Erase heading not required.)

Instructions regarding War Diaries and Intelligence Summaries are contained in F. S. Regs., Part II. and the Staff Manual respectively. Title Pages will be prepared in manuscript.

Place	Date	Hour	Summary of Events and Information	Remarks and references to Appendices
MARTINSART	26.9.15		Fine	
	27.9.15		Wet. } Very Quiet.	
	28.9.15		Showers	
	29.9.15		Wet.	
	30.9.15		At 6.40 and 8 pm tried to series of 4 rounds - at bowl 401 (Trench Mortar) in relatation. Fine	

Carruthers
Maj.
Comdg D/85. R.F.A.

85th Bdes R.7A.
Vols 8:2, 3

OCT 15

Confidential

War Diary

— of —

85th Brigade R.F.A. Hd Qrs

From 1.9.15 to 30.9.15

(Vol 1ᴬ)

Copy

Confidential

Copy

Army Form C. 2118

WAR DIARY
or
INTELLIGENCE SUMMARY

(Erase heading not required.)

Instructions regarding War Diaries and Intelligence Summaries are contained in F.S. Regs., Part II. and the Staff Manual respectively. Title Pages will be prepared in manuscript.

Place	Date	Hour	Summary of Events and Information	Remarks and references to Appendices
BONNAY	29.9.15	7 pm	H.Q. 9/85 Bde. R.F.A left BONNAY	RJW
VILLE-SUR-ANCRE	30.9.15	8.15 pm	Arrived VILLE - Bde. Commander, Area Commandant.	RJW
VILLE-SUR-ANCRE	1.9.15 to 17.9.15	4.9.15	A/85 detached from Brigade H.Q. (Joining Left Group, 18 Div. Art.) to take up position in line.	RJW
TREUX	18.9.15	10 am	H.Q. moved to TREUX - Bde. Commander appointed Area Commandant, of TREUX, MERICOURT and RIBEMONT	RJW
TREUX	19.9.15 to 30.9.15		H.Q. Still remaining at TREUX, detached from Batteries	RJW

Norrie
Lt. Col. R.F.A.
Comdg. 85 Bde. R.F.A.

1875 Wt. W593/826 1,000,000 4/15 J.B.C. & A. A.D.S.S./Forms/C. 2118.

Confidential

War Diary

of

85th Brigade R.F.A. HdQrs

From 1.10.15 to 31.10.15

(Vol. 2a)

Confidential

Army Form C. 2118

WAR DIARY
or
INTELLIGENCE SUMMARY
(Erase heading not required.)

Place	Date	Hour	Summary of Events and Information	Remarks and references to Appendices
TREUX	1.10.15		H.Q. Bde: Still remaining at TREUX, detached from Batteries which are in action.	Rgw
TREUX	2.10.15 to 31.10.15		H.Q. Bde: Still remaining at TREUX, detached from Batteries which are in action. (Nothing else to report for this month)	Rgw

R. Morphew
Lt. Col. R.F.A.
Comdg 85 Bde R.F.A.

121/7593

18th Hussars

A/85 Battery R.F.A.
Vol: 4

Oct 15

WAR DIARY
or
INTELLIGENCE SUMMARY

(Erase heading not required.)

Army Form C. 2118

Instructions regarding War Diaries and Intelligence Summaries are contained in F.S. Regs., Part II. and the Staff Manual respectively. Title Pages will be prepared in manuscript.

A BATTERY, 85TH BRIGADE
Reg. No. A/294
Date 2/11/15
ROYAL FIELD ARTILLERY

Place	Date	Hour	Summary of Events and Information	Remarks and references to Appendices
ALBERT	1st T. 3rd Oct		Fired daily into LA BOISELLE and neighbourhood in retaliation to trench mortar fire.	
	2.10.15		1 horse, 1 Rider and 1 Light Draught	
	3.10.15		1 horse, 2 Gunners joined from Base	
	26.10.15		1 Gunner posted to H.Q. 85th Bde R.F.A.	

A. Thorpharis R...
Cmdg. A/85 Bde R.F.A.

121/7593

18th Kurann

J/85 Battery R.F.A.
rot: 3

Oct/15

Army Form C. 2118

WAR DIARY
or
INTELLIGENCE SUMMARY
(Erase heading not required.)

Instructions regarding War Diaries and Intelligence Summaries are contained in F. S. Regs., Part II. and the Staff Manual respectively. Title Pages will be prepared in manuscript.

Place	Date	Hour	Summary of Events and Information	Remarks and references to Appendices
MARTINSART	1.10.15		In morning registered Point 401 from which Trench Mortar fires. In afternoon fired a few rounds at Square Tower, near Point 396. Fine day.	Ref: PLAN DIRECTEUR 2 Bis.
	2.10.15	10.15 am	The teams inspected by G.O.C. 51st Division (Gen. Harper) accompanied by C.R.A. 51st Div, at Wagon line at WARLOY - BAILLON. In morning retaliated on Trench Mortar at 401. Fired MGR	MGR
	3.10.15		From today a subaltern to remain at wagon line for periods of a week. Fine	MGR
	4.10.15		Retaliated in evening on Trench Mortar 401. Fine day.	MGR
	5.10.15		Rained all day.	MGR
	6.10.15	6. a.m	Retaliated in morning on Trench Mortars at 401, 396 ground between the Battery & MESNIL shelled heavily for a short time. Fine day	MGR
	7.10.15		Retaliated on Trench Mortar at 396 at 6.30 am & again at 11.50 pm. Misty day.	MGR
	8.10.15		Misty. Retaliated with 22 rounds on trenches at 6 pm.	MGR
	9.10.15		Dull. Fired 18 rounds at Sap at 404 about 5 pm	MGR
	10.10.15		Fine day. Retaliated on 396 & 400 at 6 pm and a combined shoot with 151st Siege at 10 pm on 404.	MGR
	11.10.15		First While registering with Shrapnel a hostile was seen to fire from Point 401. 30 Rounds Lyddite were fired at it with apparently good effect.	MGR trench mortar
	12.10.15		A new O.P was commenced this day on "JACOB'S LADDER" (communication trench between MESNIL and HAMEL in 4th Division Area). 10th Corps Summary reports that the enemy were busy during the whole of the night 11th/12th repairing parapet damaged by our fire.	MGR

Army Form C. 2118

WAR DIARY
or
INTELLIGENCE SUMMARY
(Erase heading not required.)

Instructions regarding War Diaries and Intelligence Summaries are contained in F. S. Regs., Part II. and the Staff Manual respectively. Title Pages will be prepared in manuscript.

Place	Date	Hour	Summary of Events and Information	Remarks and references to Appendices
MARTINSART	13.10.15		Gen' Geddes (C.R.A. X Corps) visits battery position. From today 6 inch Siege How's take over our task of retaliation. Rain slight.	MAP
	14.10.15		Alternative telephone lines to OPs and round battery position buried very much.	MAP
	15.10.15		Very much. Unable to see German front lines	MAP
	16.10.15		Ditto - ditto. Colonel Wylde (OC 85th Bde R.F.A.) & adjutant visited the battery	MAP
	17.10.15		Very much.	MAP
	18.10.15		In afternoon registered THIEPVAL and PIERRE-DIVION with Shrapnel. A heavy bombardment on our left. At midnight a Telephone message received warning us of a possible hostile gas attack. From today English Trench Maps taken into use	MAP REC. TRENCH MAP 57 D.S.E
	19.10.15		Major reconnoitred and chose a 2nd second gun position near BOUZINCOURT in case of retirement. Very cold and misty	MAP
	20.10.15		Misty. Unable to see.	MAP
	21.10.15		Misty	
	22.10.15		In afternoon prepared to shoot in conjunction with aeroplane, but weather too misty	
	23.10.15		Cold and fine. About 4pm fired a few rounds of Shrapnel at THIEPVAL.	
	24.10.15		Showery.	
	25.10.15		A battery position reconnoitred and chosen near HENENCOURT wood for 2nd line defence. Rain all day.	MAP
	26.10.15		Fine. At 9.45am registered cross roads behind THIEPVAL with aeroplane observation.	

Army Form C. 2118

WAR DIARY
or
INTELLIGENCE SUMMARY
(Erase heading not required.)

Instructions regarding War Diaries and Intelligence Summaries are contained in F.S. Regs., Part II. and the Staff Manual respectively. Title Pages will be prepared in manuscript.

Place	Date	Hour	Summary of Events and Information	Remarks and references to Appendices
MARTINSART	27.10.15		Fine.	REF. MAP TRENCH MAP
	28.10.15		Wet and windy. Retaliated on Square Tower R.25 b 51 in evening	MAP 57D SE
	29.10.15		Misty. Fired 3 rounds Shrapnel in retaliation in morning & at 2.30 fired at R.25. @ 9.10 added 3.45 pm at R.19 c.2.5	MAP MAP
	30.10.15		At 6 pm retaliated on R.25 c.8.7 and at 10 pm a combined shoot with 4.7 battery (6in. How's & 18 Pdrs at POZIERES (18 Rounds huddite) and again 32 rounds at 12.45 am and 8 at 2.30 am	MAP
	31.10.15		Very cold and wet. 4 Rounds retaliation at R.25 c.23 at 6 pm	MAP

Kerr Walker
Major R.F.A.
(under) R/85 Bde R.F.A.

Sect: B de: R.24.
Vol: 4

1761/121

18th Kursiur

Nov 15

"Confidential"

War Diary

of

85th Brigade R.F.A.

from 1st November to 30th November 1915

Vol. 1

Confidential —

Army Form C. 2118

WAR DIARY
or
INTELLIGENCE SUMMARY
(Erase heading not required.)

Instructions regarding War Diaries and Intelligence Summaries are contained in F.S. Regs., Part II. and the Staff Manual respectively. Title Pages will be prepared in manuscript.

Place	Date	Hour	Summary of Events and Information	Remarks and references to Appendices
TREUX	1/10/15	10 a.m	Hd Qr 85th Bde R.F.A. still @ TREUX, & detachs from Batts. which are in action	[initial]
Do	19/10/15	9 a.m	Bde: Comdr (Lt Col R.D. Whyte) proceeded to England on leave	[initial]
Do	19/10/15	9 a.m	Maj: A. Thorpe Comdg 1/85 assumed Command of 85 Bde R.F.A.	[initial]
Do	27/10/15	8 a.m	Bde Comdr (Lt Col R.D. Whyte) returned off leave	[initial]
Do	30/10/15		Hd Qr 85" Bde R.F.A. still at TREUX, detachs from Batts.	

Whyte
Lt Col R.F.A.
Comdg Br Bde R.F.A.

1875 Wt. W593/826 1,000,000 4/15 J.B.C. & A. A.D.S.S./Forms/C. 2118.

D/85 Batn
Bgra
vol. 4

D/
7656

18th Kunun

D/85 Battery

Nov. 15

Army Form C. 2118

WAR DIARY
or
INTELLIGENCE SUMMARY
(Erase heading not required.)

Instructions regarding War Diaries and Intelligence Summaries are contained in F. S. Regs., Part II. and the Staff Manual respectively. Title Pages will be prepared in manuscript.

Place	Date	Hour	Summary of Events and Information	Remarks and references to Appendices
MARTINSART	1 Nov.		Rain throughout the day	Ref: Map Sheet 57 D SE
	2 -		ditto	MAP
	3 -		Major Carruthers proceeded on leave. Tested HE shells filled with No 100 Fuze. These shell did not appear to burst well	MAP
	4th		Quiet. Fine	MAP
	5th		Retaliated in throwing to Trench Mortar at THIEPVAL. Fine	MAP
	6th		A combined shoot postponed on account of mist.	MAP
	7th		Very misty all day.	
	8th		Fired 12 rounds during the day on Trench Mortars. Germans shelled ENGELBELMER and MESNIL and AUTHUILLE, setting the former place on fire. Fine but hazy.	MAP
	9th		Retaliated on Trench Mortars. Rain in afternoon	MAP
	10th		Rain during day. Quiet	MAP
	11th		Showery. At 3.15pm fired on hostile Machine Gun enfilading our trenches from North of THIEPVAL. (R 25.c 28) Major Carruthers returned from leave.	MAP
	12th		At 1.30 pm a combined shoot took place in which we did not participate. Wet and windy.	MAP
	13th		Quiet. Fine	
	14th		Snow on ground. Fired 27 rounds in retaliation on various parts of the front. Frost and snow showers	MAP
	15th			MAP

Army Form C. 2118

WAR DIARY
or
INTELLIGENCE SUMMARY

(Erase heading not required.)

Instructions regarding War Diaries and Intelligence Summaries are contained in F.S. Regs., Part II. and the Staff Manual respectively. Title Pages will be prepared in manuscript.

Place	Date	Hour	Summary of Events and Information	Remarks and references to Appendices
MARTINSART	16th Mar		More Snow. Quiet. Lieut Godfrey proceeded on leave.	Ref. Map Sheet 57D S.E.
	17th		Thaw. Re-Registered point Q.24.b.61.	
	18th		Hard frost. Night. Quiet.	
	19th		Very windy. Quiet.	
	20th		Fired 21 rounds on Q.24.b.61 in combined shoot. Enemy retaliated with 75's on AUTHUILLE	
	21st		Frost. Left Section under Lieut Paul proceeded in evening to relieve one Section of 2nd RENFREW BTY, 3rd HIGH. BDE., in position at W.5.d.8.3.	
	22nd		Too misty to fire	
	23rd		Right Left Section registered two points in afternoon.	
	24th		Right section fired 50 rounds in re-registration. Left Section moved back to rejoin the battery at 6pm, having been relieved by 1/11 City of London How. Bde..	
	25th		Major fired 24 rounds at Machine gun emplacements, etc. One gun was reported on Machine Gun emplacement at R.31.c.30	
	26th		Combined shoot. Direct hits obtained on M.G. emplacements at R.31.c.30 and R.31.a.75. and also on houses in THIEPVAL. Germans retaliated on AUTHUILLE and marshes west of the village.	

Army Form C. 2118

WAR DIARY
or
INTELLIGENCE SUMMARY
(Erase heading not required.)

Instructions regarding War Diaries and Intelligence Summaries are contained in F. S. Regs., Part II. and the Staff Manual respectively. Title Pages will be prepared in manuscript.

Place	Date	Hour	Summary of Events and Information	Remarks and references to Appendices
MARTINSART	27th		Very hard frost. Quiet	Ref. MAP 57 D S E
	28th		ditto.	MAP
	29th		Wet. 35 rounds fired on R 31 c 30 by night to hinder working parties	MAP
	30th		Fine and Mild. fired 17 rounds in a combined shoot on R 31 c 4.9. and THIEPVAL, fired 17 rounds on R 25 c 8.6. (THIEPVAL)	MAP

Carruthers
Major, R.F.A.
Comdg. "D"/85th Bde.
R.F.A.

85th Bde: RFA.
Vol: 5

Dec 12/1938

18th/5/21

Confidential

War Diary

of

85th Brigade R.F.A.

From 1. 12. 1915 to 31. 12. 1915

Volume VI

Confidential

Army Form C. 2118

Instructions regarding War Diaries and Intelligence Summaries are contained in F.S. Regs., Part II. and the Staff Manual respectively. Title Pages will be prepared in manuscript.

WAR DIARY
INTELLIGENCE SUMMARY
(Erase heading not required.)

Place	Date	Hour	Summary of Events and Information	Remarks and references to Appendices
TREUX	1.12.15		H.Q. 85 Bde R.F.A still at TREUX. 9 detached from Batteries which are in action.	RGW
D°	10.15		Bde: Comdr assumed temporary Command of 84 "Bde R.F.A and Centre Group 18th Div. Art: He still remained in command of 85 Bde R.F.A	RGW
D°	9.2.4		Bde: Comdr resumed Sole C, command of 85 Bde R.F.A.	RGW
D°	7.12.15		Bde: Comdr assumed temporary command of 83rd Bde R.F.A and left Group 16th Div Att. He still remains in command of 85 Bde R.F.A	RGW
D°	31.12.15		H.Q. 75" Bde R.F.A still @ TREux	RGW

R.G.Wylde
Comdg 85 Bde R.F.A.

1875 Wt. W593/826 1,000,000 4/15 J.B.C. & A. A.D.S.S./Forms/C. 2118.

a/85 Salim DTg.
Vol: 6

WAR DIARY
or
INTELLIGENCE SUMMARY
(Erase heading not required.)

Army Form C. 2118

Instructions regarding War Diaries and Intelligence Summaries are contained in F.S. Regs., Part II. and the Staff Manual respectively. Title Pages will be prepared in manuscript.

Place	Date	Hour	Summary of Events and Information	Remarks and references to Appendices
Albert	1/12/15		Decrease — 1 Sgt. evacuated sick, 1 Gnr transferred 184th Tunnelling Coy, R.E. Trench Warfare	
	2/12/15		Pet. Trench Warfare RA	
	3/12/15		Pet. ditto RA	
	4/12/15		Pet. ditto RA	
	5/12/15		Trench Warfare, Ammunition Expenditure 13 Rds H.E. in Retaliation RA	
	6/12/15		— ditto — " " 8 " " " RA	
	7/12/15		— ditto — " " 3 " " Trench Warfare RA	
	8/12/15		Decrease — 1. Gnr sent back to Home Establishment — under age.	
	9/12/15		Trench Warfare, Ammunition Expenditure 20 Rds H.E. in Retaliation RA	
	10/12/15		— ditto — " " 36 " " " RA	
	11/12/15		— ditto — " " 2 " " " RA	
	12/12/15		— ditto — " " 5 " " " RA	
	13/12/15		— ditto — " " 30 " " " RA	
	14/12/15		Trench Warfare Ammunition Expenditure 35 Rds H.E. in Retaliation RA	
	15/12/15		— ditto — " " 3 " " " RA	
	16/12/15		Decrease — Major A. Thorp, posted to 82nd Bde, R.F.A, on promotion to Lt. Col. Trench Warfare	
	17/12/15		— " — 1. Gnr & 1. Driver " " " " RA	
	18/12/15		Trench Warfare Ammunition Expenditure 4 Rds H.E. in Retaliation. RA	
			— ditto — " " 53 " " " RA	
			— ditto — " " 28 " " " RA	
	19/12/15		— ditto — " " 34 " " " RA	

Army Form C. 2118

WAR DIARY
or
INTELLIGENCE SUMMARY
(Erase heading not required.)

Instructions regarding War Diaries and Intelligence Summaries are contained in F.S. Regs., Part II. and the Staff Manual respectively. Title Pages will be prepared in manuscript.

Place	Date	Hour	Summary of Events and Information	Remarks and references to Appendices
Albert	20/12/15		Trench Warfare, Ammunition Expenditure 89 Rds H.E. in Retaliation. RA	
	21/12/15		2/L Trench Warfare RA	
	22/12/15		2/L Trench Warfare RA	
	23/12/15		2/L Trench Warfare RA	
	24/12/15		Trench Warfare, Ammunition Expenditure 11 Rds Shrapnel RA	
	25/12/15		ditto 1 " 8 " " RA	
	26/12/15		Decrease — 1. T/L transferred to French Mortar School (Gft Pommer). Trench Warfare RA	
	27/12/15		2/L Trench Warfare RA	
	28/12/15		Increase — 1 Gunner posted from 85 & 2nd R.F.A. B/L. Trench Warfare RA	
	29/12/15		Trench Warfare, Ammunition Expenditure 11 Rds H.E. in Retaliation. RA	
	30/12/15		— ditto — " 41 " " " " RA	
	30/12/15		— ditto — " 5 " Shrapnel " " RA	
	31/12/15		— ditto — " 8 " H.E. in Retaliation. RA	

R.M.French Capt. RA
R.F.A.
COMDG. A/85th BRIGADE R.F.A.

18th Kisrolor

13/85 Dahin
Vol 6

121/7809

Decr 15

CONFIDENTIAL.

WAR DIARY
OF
"B" BATTERY 85TH BDE R.F.A.

FROM 1ST DECEMBER TO 31ST DECR 1915

(VOLUME VI).

WAR DIARY or INTELLIGENCE SUMMARY

Army Form C. 2118

B Battery 85th Bde R.F.A.

(Erase heading not required.)

Instructions regarding War Diaries and Intelligence Summaries are contained in F.S. Regs., Part II. and the Staff Manual respectively. Title Pages will be prepared in manuscript.

Place	Date	Hour	Summary of Events and Information	Remarks and references to Appendices
FRANCE. BRAY-SUR SOMME	1/XII		All the beginning of the month the battery was still in action in the same position in a valley 1 mile N of BRAY-SUR-SOMME. The old targets were registered and the battery was in constant communication with forward observing posts in D1 & D2 sector. Some trouble was experienced owing to falls in the roof of the gun-pit passage and further work was done in lagging and strutting to consolidate these passages. The weather was wet and owing to the clayey and chalky nature of the soil, water found its way to the gun-pits. This caused the pits to be wet and measures had to be taken to drain off the leakage by means of a false interior ceiling of corrugated iron sheeting and the digging of sumps in the floor. Owing to the wet state of the telephone wires and crumbling in of existing trenches large portions of this wiring had to be removed being replaced by simple ground wires running near the trenches. Gun telephone exchange.—	SJV
	14/XII		The one man duty Rangefinder. Barr & Stroud Mk I was adjusted by the staff artificer.	SJV
	16/XII		The construction of a new telephone exchange dugout, between B & C gunpits, in order to maintain better control of the battery whilst firing, was decided upon.	SJV

Army Form C. 2118

WAR DIARY
or
~~INTELLIGENCE SUMMARY~~ 'B' Battery 85th Bde R.F.A.

(Erase heading not required.)

Instructions regarding War Diaries and Intelligence Summaries are contained in F.S. Regs., Part II. and the Staff Manual respectively. Title Pages will be prepared in manuscript.

Place	Date 1915.	Hour	Summary of Events and Information	Remarks and references to Appendices
FRANCE. BRAY-SUR-SOMME.	29/XII	5.40 p.m.	Owing to the use by the enemy of gas shells the battery was ordered to 'STAND-TO' for about 1½ hours as a precautionary measure.	J.XII
MEAULTE	1/XII	—	The wagon line remained in the same billets at MEAULTE, work being done by fatigue parties to improve the accommodation by repairing old buildings, the erection of a new stable, and the paving of pathways with bricks. Great scarcity of men to carry on work in the battery —	

1875. Wt. W593/826 1,000,000 4/15 J.B.C. & A. A.D.S.S./Forms/C. 2118.

8/85 Bombay
Vol: 5

12/7795

18th Kurrum

Recs 15.

Army Form C. 2118

WAR DIARY
or
INTELLIGENCE SUMMARY
(Erase heading not required.)

Instructions regarding War Diaries and Intelligence Summaries are contained in F.S. Regs., Part II. and the Staff Manual respectively. Title Pages will be prepared in manuscript.

Place	Date	Hour	Summary of Events and Information	Remarks and references to Appendices
MARTINSART	1.12.15		Wet. Slight rain and misty. No firing. Position in AUTHUILLE WOOD reconnoitred for *das shooting*	MP
	2.12.15		Wet. A fatigue party dug gun pit at W 6 d 57 for *das shooting*	REF OVILLERS & BEAUMONT TRENCH MAP 2nd Edit 57D SE 4 & 57D SE 1
	3.12.15		A gun taken into position at 5 a.m. for wire cutting. Shoot postponed owing to mist.	MP
	4.12.15		At 2 p.m. fire was opened by all batteries in the sector. D185 opened on R.31.c.31, R.31.c.98 & R.31.A.7.8, several direct hits being obtained. A gun fired 24 rounds of H.E. Fuze 100 at earth works at A.31.c.2110 at range of 800 yards. Several shells ricochetted. 5th charge was used. Gun removed the same evening. Right Section under LIEUT PAUL relieved 1/1 City of London How Bty T.F. at gun position at W 5 d 72, coming 300 from X 1 a 8382 to OVILLERS	MP
	5.12.15		Rain and windy. D185 retaliated with a few rounds. Detached section commenced registration	MP
	6.12.15		The battery fired about 25 rounds at R.19.c.25 and Q.18.a.38, being part of an arranged programme. Detached action continued registration	MP
	7.12.15		The battery fired 30 rounds at A.25.b.38 & A.25.b.23. Detached action continued registration. Rain in afternoon.	MP
	8.12.15		Fine. Battery fired 26 rounds with good effect on M.G. emplacements at R 31 a 75 and R 31 a 53. Detached action continued registration. Three officers from 41st Div! Artillery attached from 1st day for instruction. At HQ with the battery. LIEUTS BURLEIGH and SIMPSEN to the Section	MP

Army Form C. 2118

WAR DIARY
or
INTELLIGENCE SUMMARY

(Erase heading not required.)

Instructions regarding War Diaries and Intelligence Summaries are contained in F. S. Regs, Part II. and the Staff Manual respectively. Title Pages will be prepared in manuscript.

Place	Date	Hour	Summary of Events and Information	Remarks and references to Appendices
MARTINSART & AVELUY.	9.12.15		Rain all day. 4 rounds fired by battery on R31c49 in retaliation to trench mortar	MAP
	10.12.15		No firing. Fine.	
	11.12.15		Section continued registration. ALBERT, AVELUY and MARTINSART shelled heavily at intervals throughout the night. Two chargers stabled in MARTINSART hut. One killed.	MAP
	12.12.15		Fine. Battery fired 38 rounds at M.G. emplacements at R31 a 42. 1 Section 2nd RENFREW came into action at AVELUY POSN.	MAP
	13.12.15		Fine and frosty. German aerial activity. Battle plane seen in morning.	MAP
	14.12.15		Fine. Section ordered to return to Battery postion 'A' gun to go into prepared postion at	MAP
			W6d 57 few were cutting experiment. Guns moved in the dark. 'B' gun went into postion	
	15.12.15		at Q34 b 43 for wire cutting at R19 c 25. Fire opened at 2.0 p.m., the other batteries of the sector joining in	MAP
			experiment attached 180 rounds fired in all 'A' & 'B' guns withdrawn to gun postion in evening. Report on wire cutting	Appendix A
	16.12.15		Fine. Quiet day. Lieut JONES proceeded on leave.	MAP
	17.12.15		Fine. Fired a few rounds in retaliation.	MAP
	18.12.15		Fine. Quiet.	
	19.12.15		Fine and frosty. 25 rounds fired with good effect at M.G. emplacement R19 c15. Attached officers returned to England.	MAP
	20.12.15		Major CARRUTHERS takes over command of Left Group vice Col. MUDIE (on leave)	MAP
	21.12.15		Rain and mist. Quiet. A gun taken to W6 d 57.	
	22.12.15		Wet. Genl GEDDES (CRA 10th Corps) Genl McCARTHY (BGA 51st Div) & CRA (53rd Div) inspected gun postion. Quiet.	MAP

Army Form C. 2118

WAR DIARY
or
INTELLIGENCE SUMMARY
(Erase heading not required.)

Instructions regarding War Diaries and Intelligence Summaries are contained in F.S. Regs., Part II. and the Staff Manual respectively. Title Pages will be prepared in manuscript.

Place	Date	Hour	Summary of Events and Information	Remarks and references to Appendices
MARTINSART	23.12.15		Raining. Quiet.	NIL
	24.12.15		Fine. At 1.30 pm organised shoot commenced, on German trenches from THIEPVAL to X.1.a.8.3&2., and again at 2.30 pm. Battery under LIEUT GODFREY fired at R.31.c.4.5. A gun fired at wire at R.31.c.2.5c.5. LIEUT JONES returning from leave. Germans fired about 30 shells at MARTINSART at 3.45 pm doing no damage. Fine and Quiet.	Appendix 13.12 NIL NIL
	26.12.15		At 11.30 am fired 30 rounds at ST PIERRE DIVION. Germans retaliated on HAMEL. Very windy, but fine.	NIL
	27.12.15		Ammunition allotment to coming weeks NIL. One officer & gunner arrived from 1st RENFREW for instruction.	NIL
	28.12.15		Fine. Organised shoot at 2.30. 1st RENFREW fired with 2 guns from near MESNIL. We did not fire.	NIL
	29.12.15		Quiet & fine.	NIL
	30.12.15		MAJOR CARRUTHERS assumed command of the battery.	NIL
	31.12.15		Fine and quiet.	NIL

Maxwell
Maj.
OC 5785

A

Report on Wire cutting at R.31.C.30. by a Single 4.5 How^r on 15-12-15

The Gun was placed in a prepared pit at the N. end of a ride through AUTHUILLE (W.6.d 57) with a view to cutting the wire in front of the German trenches at R.31.C 30.

This point was chosen because.

(i) a good view of the wire could be obtained from the front line trench.

(ii) the observer is in the line of fire thus facilitating observation

The Wire   The wire at this point appears to be from 30′ to 40′ broad & in good condition. It is supported on wooded posts near the hostile trench, and on iron railing standards on the side nearest our trenches.

Fire was opened at 2 p.m. the first round falling in the German wire just left of the point chosen. From the fourth round onwards effective fire was opened on the desired point

2.

The first thirty pounds were fired on or about the same line, and cut a way through almost to German parapet.

The gun was then turned on 6 yards to the left and a similar effect was produced.

On carefully examining the wire after the shoot was over it appeared.

(I) that the wire had been damaged on a front of from 10 to 15 yards.

(II) that on the whole of this front the iron standards were either lying on the ground or else inclined.

(III) that on the right a way appeared to be cut almost to the German parapet, where there were still a few posts and some wire intact.

(IV) that in the centre, except for the front iron posts, the wire and posts were very slightly damaged.

(V) that the effect on the left was similar to that on the right but the damage done was not so complete.

Gunnery.   3.

The gun shot most accurately although owing to the state of the ground the left wheel sank considerably, although a foundation of broken bricks had previously been prepared.

Only two shells failed to explode.

One shell ricochetted.

After the thirtieth round the shells began to drop a yard or so short and small elevations of a minute had to be given.

The laying was done by means of a post in front for line, and by the sight clinometer for elevation.

(SIGNED) L.I.C. PAUL
II/35 Bde RH

B‡

REPORT on wire cutting carried out by a single 4.5 Howitzer
II/85 RFA

PRELIMINARY

An experiment was carried out by a 4.5 Howitzer in cutting wire with:-
   a) Percussion Shrapnel.
   b) HE Fuze 44.
   c) HE Fuze 100.
Delay Action.

Position of Gun, Target & Observer

The gun was situated in a prepared pit at W6 II 5.7 at the end of a ride.

The wire to be cut was at R31 c 25 05.

The observer was in the front line trench at X.1.a 15 this making observation easier, being in line of fire.

The Wire.

The wire at this point was about 9 yards broad, fairly thick and appeared in good condition.

It was supported on iron railings in front and on stout wooden stakes behind.

Shrapnel

At 1.30 pm fire was opened with Percussion Shrapnel 5th Charge. The first round fell in the wire just to the left of the target.

From the 2nd round effective fire was opened and sixteen rounds in all fired.

Effect

A clear way was cut through to the enemy's parapet, the wire being cut and the posts blown or pulled down. The gap appeared to be about two yards broad.

H.E. Fuze 44.

Next 20 pounds of H.E. (Trotyl + TNT) fitted with No 44 Fuze were fired. Of these 4 rounds were blind.

Effect

These shell were fired on the right of the gap made by the Shrapnel. The effect appeared to be that the

3.

wire was not much cut, but it was blown up attached to the stakes, and remained in coils and bundles near where it originally stood.

They would thus still form an obstacle.

H E FUZE 100. Delay Action	20 pounds of HE fitted with the No 100 fuze were then fired. Of these about 8 ricochetted up through the wire, bursting beyond it and doing no damage to the wire
Effect. HE Fuze. 100	These shells appeared to have very little effect on the wire, doing less damage than those fitted with Fuze 44.
Summary.	From this experiment it would appear that Percussion Shrapnel gives a far better result than shells filled with HE

[Attached are some Gunnery Notes on this and previous experiments]

(SIGNED) L.I.C. PAUL. LIEUT
II/85 Bde RFA

B 1

Gunnery Notes

Platform.

In former experiments from this position it had been found that:—

I. A platform of wooden logs (diam about 2") laid parallel to the axle was no good. The gun "side-shifted" in spite of sandbags placed behind the wheels. The left wheel finally slipped off the platform and sank in the soft earth. [There had been a ditch on this side previously.]

The shooting was inaccurate.

II. A platform of broken bricks, 4 inches deep was next tried. The left wheel forced a way through the bricks and sank.

Although this wheel sunk almost up to the axle, the shooting was most accurate, the cross level being adjusted throughout the shoot.

III. On this occasion a hole about 2 foot deep, 1 foot broad and 3 ft long was dug where each wheel would rest. The bottom was lined with wood & the hole was then filled in with broken bricks closely packed together.
   This platform answered well

The Spade on all three occasions was allowed to bury itself in the ground — which was composed of gravel

LAYING

The laying was done by means of a front aiming post for line and by the Sight Clinometer for Elevation the Range Drum being zero. It was first checked by Field Clinometer

The total Elevation of the Gun was 3° 20', of which 1° 15' was allowed for the angle of sight to the target
   The Angle of Sight to the crest of the hill, about 400 to 500 yds distant was 2° 45' Elev

Laying could Differences of 1 minute for elevation and 2½ minutes for deflection, although naturally not put on absolutely accurately, showed an appreciable alteration in the spot where the shell fell.

Flash. A flash screen, 10 ft high and 20 ft long composed of brushwood and leaves, was placed on the right of the gun, to prevent any chance of the flash being seen through the trees of the wood; from trenches about 1200 yds. on the right flank.

When standing on the same level as the top of the shield one could see the German wire.

On looking back from the front line trench towards the gun, no flash could be seen when it fired, but the shell could be observed in its flight.

"5th Charge" was used throughout. The Cartridges were Ballistite.

(SIGNED) L.J.C. PAUL. LIEUT.
II/85 Bde. R.F.A.

85th Bde. RFA.
Vol. 6

JAN 16

18

Confidential
War Diary
of
75th Brigade R.F.A. H.Q.

From 1st Jany 1916 to 31.12.16

Vol III

Confidential

Army Form C. 2118

WAR DIARY
or
INTELLIGENCE SUMMARY
(Erase heading not required.)

Instructions regarding War Diaries and Intelligence Summaries are contained in F.S. Regs., Part II. and the Staff Manual respectively. Title Pages will be prepared in manuscript.

Place	Date	Hour	Summary of Events and Information	Remarks and references to Appendices
TREUX	1.1.16		H.Q. 85th & 8th R.F.A. Still @ TREUX & detaches from Batteries which arm action	RJW
Do	2.1.16		Bde. Comd. returned to Bde. H.Q. from temporary Command of Left Group	RJW
Do	10.1.16		Bde: Comd: on Command at BEAUVAL	RJW
Do	15.1.16		Bde: Comd: returned from BEAUVAL	RJW
Do	19.1.16		2/85 turn out of billets at SUZE — rejoined 85 Bde Bt.	RJW
Do	20.1.16		Capt Roche took over Command of B.B.A.C.	RJW
Do	21.1.16		Capt ALMACK A/85. Killed in action. Lieut Paul assumed temporary command of A/85	RJW
Do	30.1.16		Capt Lockhart took over Command of A/85	RJW

Roushe
Comdg 85 RGA
1st to 31st

13/85 Battery
rd: 7

JHN

CONFIDENTIAL

WAR DIARY

OF

'B' BATTERY 85TH BDE R.F.A.

FROM 1ST JANUARY 1916 TO 31ST JANUARY 1916

(VOLUME VII.)

Army Form C. 2118

WAR DIARY
or
INTELLIGENCE SUMMARY
(Erase heading not required.)

B Battery 85th Bde
R.F.A.

Place	Date	Hour	Summary of Events and Information	Remarks and references to Appendices
BRAY-SUR-SOMME	1/1/16	—	The battery remained in action in the same position. Whilst not actually engaged in firing, the men of this battery were engaged on fatigues etc. to improve the position and instruction in gun drill etc was given to accustom the gunners to work under difficulties e.g. whilst wearing goggles or smoke helmets. Progress was made with the construction of a new telephone hut between B & C gunpits. Work was also done on new wire trenches to forward observation posts. Broken track and rubble was drawn from ALBERT and used to repair the floors of the gun-pits and passages. Rubble was also used to form a footpath through a particularly muddy part of the position. Progress was also made with the construction of an officer's dugout.	S.H.
	19/1	noon	A premature occurred when using AMATOL 40/60 with N.0.4 gun, several pieces of shell were blown back into the gun pit, one gunner being very slightly wounded.	S.H.
	26/1	2 pm	The new telephone exchange was completed and occupied by the operators.	S.H.
	26/1	4 pm	Enemy fired 9 shells (in 3 salvos) probably from a 5" gun, the rounds falling near the gun-pits of right section.	S.H.
	27/1	11.45 am	Three more rounds were fired by hostile artillery, the rounds falling as before.	S.H.

WAR DIARY
or
INTELLIGENCE SUMMARY

B Battery 85th Bde
R.F.A.

Army Form C. 2118

(Erase heading not required.)

Place	Date 1916	Hour	Summary of Events and Information	Remarks and references to Appendices
BRAY. SUR. SOMME	28/1	10 a.m.	A further twelve rounds fell near the right section gun pits but no damage was done to the battery.	
	3/1		Shell traces of two rounds the Battery and the opportunity was taken to register the Battery in case during a gas attack.	
MEAULTE	1/30 N.	-	The WAGON LINE remained at MEAULTE Besides the ordinary work of a wagon line, fatigue parties constructed a battery wash house and drying room.	

C/85 Bakery
Vol: 48 4

WAR DIARY or INTELLIGENCE SUMMARY

Army Form C. 2118

C/85 RFA

Place	Date	Hour	Summary of Events and Information	Remarks and references to Appendices
Meaulte	4.1.16		Wirecutting experiment carried out at 3 pm from a position prepared at F29 0075 by A gun at range of 1450 yds at wire at X20d 7028. 30 Percussion Shrapnel including a few slow Air bursts - also 10 HE with fuze 44. The shoot was not very satisfactory as platform was too soft. Up wheel and up in also however inconsiderable - The Percussion were more effective on the wire - HE on the parapet no plug.	
	7/8/1/16 mid N		A bombing attack from TAMBOUR by East Surreys was planned for 1 am when bombing attack started. The O.C. Infantry orders Fire - the batteries to fire till 3 am. but scheme fell through as the bombers on the the batteries stood by till 3 am. but scheme fell through as the bombers on the left started before main attack was in position at F3a 61 -	
	8.1.16	6 pm	At 5.30 pm the E. Surreys made another demonstration at this point to entice the Germans on to their parados which we suspected to occupy in case of a bombing attack. At 6 pm C/85 fired 40 rds BX at trenches from F3c 69 - F3a 64 in conjunction with the field batteries.	
	7.1.16		C/164 RFA came up to be attached to the battery for training - occupied the alternative position of registered one section on a quickly vacated -	
	19.1.16 12.1.16		BAD gunpits rebuilt, completed & put in a continuous slope to roof - Shelled dugouts behind HIDDEN WOOD 25 rds BX.	at 11.20 avialling A of 11.20
			Continued firing shoot at 11 am at NORD Sap F3a 49 - 12 rapid rounds ex BX at same pt. at 11.25 fire lifted to corner of Willow (30 more 120 BX - 120 BX. Shoot Magnificent. Inf. Engineer reported afterwards. Been effective.	
	16.1.16		20 BX fired at MG emplacement at F3c 572, effective. Enemy to retaliate on all Vague line at BUIRE though made a fixed target. Attachment last week 140 BX 14 B.	

Army Form C. 2118

C/85 WAR DIARY
R.F.A.
or
INTELLIGENCE SUMMARY
(Erase heading not required.)

Place	Date	Hour	Summary of Events and Information	Remarks and references to Appendices
Meault	18th	10:30	The Germans had been shelling BECORDEL a good deal lately when they commenced doing so at about 10:30 am we retaliated firing on ROSE COTTAGE obtaining 10 direct hits. Considerable damage was done to the inside & section of the house. The Germans have not shelled BECORDEL since.	
	18th		C/164 RFA withdrawn from alternative position.	
	22nd		Confined group shoot at 11:30am by A, B, D/84 and C/85 at ahy eml in Support trench at X 26d 98x at trench communication trench t5 LOZENGE WOOD - Shooting very accurate - Total rounds 63 Bx.	
			Allotment for week 140 Bx. Balance expended on machine guns & registration.	
			Yr Ws Neilson attached to uplace Yr Hewitt temporarily sick returned on 28th	
	22		3's Bx fired on front trenches each hour at F.3.6.t.3. to check	
	28		3's Bx Bx fired 26's Bx reputation also on machine gun in house in FRICOURT. allotment 192 Bx 10 B. fired 26's Bx	
	31		after a bombardment from 11:30 am during which we retaliated occasionally orders were received to fire 50 rds Bx at 3:30 P.M. at trench from F.3.a. 6.0.25 - F.3.a. 45.50 being the front trench of front the TAMBOU R. which had been heavily shelling with C.D. We repeated with another 50 rds Bx at 4:10 PM - 4:20 PM. The enemy retaliated slightly but at about 5:0 PM they turned a [illegible] [illegible] [illegible] perceptible at the battery at 5:15 PM. This was accompanied by heavy [illegible] find hyperifically on F.[illegible] [sector]. This [illegible] accommodated [illegible] fell about [illegible] F.4 [illegible] [illegible] [illegible] about gas rate of the F.4 trenches of F. Pendelson 20

1875 Wt. W 593/826 1,000,000 4/15 J.B.C. & A. A.D.S.S./Forms/C. 2118.

8/85 Battery Pra.
Vol 6
Jan '16

Army Form C. 2118

WAR DIARY
or
INTELLIGENCE SUMMARY
(Erase heading not required.)

Instructions regarding War Diaries and Intelligence Summaries are contained in F. S. Regs., Part II. and the Staff Manual respectively. Title Pages will be prepared in manuscript.

Place	Date	Hour	Summary of Events and Information	Remarks and references to Appendices
MARTINSART	1.1.16		Windy + wet. Quiet day. T.J.	
	2.1.16		Wet day. T.J.	
	3.1.16		Fine day. T.J.	
	4.1.16		LIEUT PAUL proceeds on leave. T.J.	
	5.1.16		Fine. Germans fired about 50 5.9 shells at MESNIL in morning, and about 20 more in afternoon. T.J.	
	6.1.16		Wet. T.J.	
	7.1.16		Wet. T.J.	
	8.1.16		The battery relieved by B Battery, 164th Bde. Major CARROTHERS is to remain for a short time in command of relieving Battery with LIEUT JONES, 1 N.C.O. and of signallers. The rest that is command of Right Section back in the morning to begin line at WARLOY-BAILLON. T.J.	
			GODFREY takes Right Section into WARLOY-BAILLON. T.J.	
			Light section of the new Battery comes in 7.30 P.M. T.J.	
			& the Left Section goes back to Wagon lines in the evening. T.J.	
	9.1.16		Fine. Left Section goes back to Wagon lines in the evening. T.J.	
	10.1.16		T.J.	
	11.1.16		MAJOR CARROTHERS assumes command of 85th Bde R.F.A. while Col. WYLDE is away. T.J.	
	12.1.16		T.J.	
	13.1.16		T.J.	
	14.1.16		T.J.	
	15.1.16		MAJOR CARROTHERS relinquishes command of 85th Bde. Col. WYLDE having returned. T.J.	
	16.1.16		LIEUT PAUL returns off leave. T.J.	
	17.1.16		T.J.	
	18.1.16		MAJOR CARROTHERS relinquishes command of 'B'/164th Bde & rejoins battery. T.J.	
WARLOY BAILLON	19.1.16		T.J.	

1875 Wt. W593/826 1,000,000 4/15 J.B.C. & A. A.D.S.S./Forms/C. 2118.

Army Form C. 2118

WAR DIARY
or
INTELLIGENCE SUMMARY

(Erase heading not required.)

Instructions regarding War Diaries and Intelligence Summaries are contained in F. S. Regs., Part II. and the Staff Manual respectively. Title Pages will be prepared in manuscript.

Place	Date	Hour	Summary of Events and Information	Remarks and references to Appendices
MARLOY-BAILLON	20.1.16		Battery rejoins 18th Division & proceeds to BUIRE. T.J.	
BUIRE	21.1.16		T.J.	
	22.1.16		Inst. Maven T.J.	
	23.1.16		T.J.	
	24.1.16		T.J.	
	25.1.16		LIEUT PAUL leaves to command 'A' 85th Bde vice Capt ALMACK killed. T.J.	
	26.1.16		T.J.	
	27.1.16		T.J.	
	28.1.16		T.J.	
	29.1.16		T.J.	
	30.1.16		T.J.	
	31.1.16		MAJOR CARROTHERS reconnoitres new position T.J.	

Neville Major
Comdg B/85 R.F.A.

Confidential

War Diary

of

85th Brigade. R.F.A. H.d Q.rs

From 1.2.16   To 29.2.16

Volume (IV)

Confidential

WAR DIARY
INTELLIGENCE SUMMARY
(Erase heading not required.)

Army Form C. 2118

Place	Date	Hour	Summary of Events and Information	Remarks and references to Appendices
TREUX	1.2.16	12 am	H.Q. still at TREUX	RW
LAVIEVILLE	2.2.16	12 noon	H.Q. moved to LAVIEVILLE — a small rather delapidated village one or two good dwellings however at the South end of it. At the North end of village a good water can be obtained of ALBERT on a clear day. A pumping station has been erected by R.E.'s in centre of village. Six capacious tanks placed nearly on the local EAP is almost unfit for human consumption. Beds have been erected in all available barns by the R.E.'s + a considerable number of Troops can be accommodated to meet food corn for the use of the village. Lieut. Colonel Combe appointed Area Commandant & Adjutant Lieut. Major	RW
Do	6.2.16		85. B.A.C. moved to LAVIEVILLE	RW
Do	6.2.16		6/85 moved to LAVIEVILLES offr coming 1 broken, out of action	RW
Do	8.2.16		8/85 late personnel + horses transferred to 85 Dn. also 19 men 28 horses 9 A.M. Cadre of the 85. B.A.C. 6 + D. Batts: nomenclature unaltered through the note.	RW
Do	29/2/16		H.Q. 6/85 85 BAC 87th @ LAVIEVILLE	RW

29.2.16.

Lt.Col. J.R.F.A.
Comdg 8th Bde R.F.A.

Vol.12

FEB

A BTY

85TH BDE.
R.F.A.

WAR DIARY or INTELLIGENCE SUMMARY

Army Form C. 2118

Place	Date	Hour	Summary of Events and Information	Remarks and references to Appendices
ALBERT	1/2/16		Ammunition expended 20 rds BX. Decrease 1 officers charger. Increase 2 Lt PARKER posted from 85th B.A.C. NWB	Ref map. French OVILLERS 57 D SE 4
	2/2/16		Fired 13 B and 4 BX. Quiet. NWB	
	3/2/16		Nothing to report. NWB	
	4/2/16		Bombardment from 11am to 1pm and from 3pm to 5pm of enemy's trenches in X20a. 120 rounds BX. CAPT LOCKHART posted to 36th Div. Arty. LIEUT PAUL assumed command. NWB	
	5/2/16		Bombardment from 3.15 to 4pm at communication trenches at X14 c4509, X20 a8279, X20 B38 X20 A9547. 120 rounds BX fired. NWB	
	6/2/16		10.25pm retaliated with 4 BX to Trench Mortars. 2 Lieut FENTON proceeded on leave to England. NWB	
	7/2/16		Quiet day. NWB	
	8/2/16		10 Rounds BX registration. Clear day. 5 Hostile Balloons up along German front in view of the Battery. NWB	
	9/2/16		Snow during the day. All quiet. NWB	
	10/2/16		11 Rounds BX registration. Lieut PAUL granted temporary rank of captain. NWB	
	11/2/16		Raining all quiet. Retaliated with 8 rounds BX to Trench Mortars in evening. NWB	
	12/2/16		35 Rounds BX registration. NWB	

WAR DIARY or INTELLIGENCE SUMMARY

Army Form C. 2118

Place	Date	Hour	Summary of Events and Information	Remarks and references to Appendices
ALBERT	13/7/16		Hostile Trench mortars active in LA BOISELLE. We fired during the day 42 rounds in retaliation. Also 14 rounds in registration. AAA	Reference FRENCH MAP TRENCH MAP OVILLERS 57.D Sheet 4
	14/7/16		From 3:30 pm to 4:5 pm retaliated with 43 rounds BX on Trench Mortar position at X14 c 00. AAA	
	15/7/16	12:30 pm	Fired at working party at R 33 c with 8 rounds B. a defensive fire. AAA. Lieut FENTON returned from leave. AAA	
	16/7/16		From 4 pm to 4:50 pm, after registration, fired 120 rounds BX on trenches from X8c55 to X8c53 in co-operation with bombardment carried out by 32nd Div on our left. AAA. 13 Rounds BX registration. 3pm. 12 rounds retaliation to T Mortars. AAA	
	17/7/16			
	18/7/16	4:10 pm	Fired on Trench Mortars at X13D63 – 9 Rounds BX. AAA	
	19/7/16		30 Rounds BX during day at Trench Mortars, active in LA BOISELLE. AAA	
	20/7/16		During morning fired 61 rounds BX on X14 c 28, X14c 89, X20 A 55 in retaliation to hostile shelling of X13 c 42 by 4.2" Hows. AAA. S/M YOAK is gazetted to a commission. AAA	
	21/7/16		Deargaze Sgt. Major YOAK to England on gazetting to a commission. AAA. 49 round BX in afternoon, registration & retaliation to Trench Mortars	
	22/7/16		Fired 16 rounds retaliation to Trench Mortars in BOISELLE at 6.20 pm. Heavy Bombardment by Germans of TAMBOUR. AAA	

WAR DIARY
or
INTELLIGENCE SUMMARY

(Erase heading not required.)

Army Form C. 2118

Place	Date	Hour	Summary of Events and Information	Remarks and references to Appendices
ALBERT	23/2/16		All quiet. Showing all day	Reference Trench Map BILLERS STD SE"
	24/2/16		ditto LIEUT HAYBITTEL (adjt 8th H.Q.) attached MAP	
	25/2/16		2 Lieut T.B. KEYMS attached to the Battery from England MAP	
	26/2/16		Lieut T.B. KEYMS attached to the Battery from England hd. MAP	
	27/2/16		4.10 pm. 12 Rounds B X at X13 D 6 5 4 5 in retaliation to grenades & bombs from LA BOISELLE MAP	
	28/2/16		Fired 36 Round BX in retaliation to Trench Mortars MAP	
	29/2/16		Lieut HAYBITTEL rejoined 8sth. Headquarters. Fired 17 rounds BX into LA BOISELLE in retaliation to Trench Mortars. Heavy Bombardment about 6pm on our right MAP	

B. Battery
8s & Bde
R.F.A.
1823
Vol. 8

CONFIDENTIAL

25.2.16

WAR DIARY

OF

'B' BATTERY 85TH BDE R.F.A.

FROM 1ST FEBRUARY TO 29TH FEB 1916.

(VOLUME VIII).

Army Form C. 2118

WAR DIARY
or
INTELLIGENCE SUMMARY

(Erase heading not required.)

Instructions regarding War Diaries and Intelligence Summaries are contained in F. S. Regs., Part II. and the Staff Manual respectively. Title Pages will be prepared in manuscript.

Place	Date	Hour	Summary of Events and Information	Remarks and references to Appendices

1875 Wt. W593/826 1,000,000 4/15 J.B.C. & A. A.D.S.S./Forms/C. 2118.

Army Form C. 2118

WAR DIARY
or
INTELLIGENCE SUMMARY
(Erase heading not required.)

B Battery. 85th Bde R.F.A.

Instructions regarding War Diaries and Intelligence Summaries are contained in F.S. Regs., Part II. and the Staff Manual respectively. Title Pages will be prepared in manuscript.

Place	Date 1916	Hour	Summary of Events and Information	Remarks and references to Appendices
BRAY-SUR-SOMME	1/II	-	The Battery remained in action in the same position 1 mile N of BRAY-SUR-SOMME. The gunners and battery staff being engaged in their usual duties.	
MEAULTE	2/II	-	The Wagon line was moved from MEAULTE to BUIRE-SUR-L'ANCRE.	
BRAY-SUR-SOMME	6/II	7pm	The right section (No 1 & 2 guns) moved out from the position, the gun pits and dugouts being taken over by the 7th Divisional Artillery	
	7/II	7.30 pm	The left section and battery staff left the position and billetted for the night at the Wagon line at BUIRE-SUR-L'ANCRE.	
BUIRE-SUR-L'ANCRE	8/II	10 am	The battery marched by road from BUIRE-SUR-L'ANCRE to TALMAS via BEAUCOURT-SUR-L'HALLUE.	
TALMAS	9/II	9am	The battery marched by road from TALMAS to FRANSU where it joined the 4th WEST LANCS (HOWITZER) BRIGADE. R.F.A. (55TH DIVISIONAL ARTILLERY).	

Army Form C. 2118

WAR DIARY
or
INTELLIGENCE SUMMARY
(Erase heading not required.)

B Battery 85th Bde R.F.A.

Place	Date 1916	Hour	Summary of Events and Information	Remarks and references to Appendices
FRANCE				
FRANSU	9/11	—	The battery joined the 4th WEST LANCS. (HOW) BRIGADE R.F.A which formed part of the 55th DIVISIONAL ARTILLERY.	S.S.J
	11/11	8am	The battery marched as part of the brigade from FRANSU to HALLOY by road to HALLOY the horses were accommodated in a field and the men in canvas huts near by.	R.S.J
HALLOY	12/11	8am	The battery marched from HALLOY to COUTURELLE arriving about noon.	S.S.J
COUTURELLE	14/11	9am	A party of N.C.O's and gunners proceeded to a position in GROSVILLE in the commune of RIVIERE to prepare gun platforms, the remainder of the battery being billeted in COUTURELLE.	S.S.J
	16/11	9am	The battery marched from COUTURELLE to MONCHIET the position allotted as the battery wagon line.	R.S.J
MONCHIET			The left section guns were placed in position at GROSVILLE in the commune of RIVIERE and registration of targets commenced.	
	24/11	—	The right section guns were placed in position at GROSVILLE on temporary gun platforms and registration commenced.	S.S.J

E.S.M. Cummins HR.F.A

C. Ball
85 F.F.A.
18" Dis
Vol. 3

FEB

WAR DIARY
INTELLIGENCE SUMMARY
(Erase heading not required.)

Army Form C. 2118

February

Instructions regarding War Diaries and Intelligence Summaries are contained in F.S. Regs., Part II. and the Staff Manual respectively. Title Pages will be prepared in manuscript.

Place	Date	Hour	Summary of Events and Information	Remarks and references to Appendices
Meaulte	4/2/16	—	After 3 quiet days orders were received to co-operate in an attack by the French at FRISE & the bends from M.1 & 60 at F.11.b.39.03. to F.11.b.55.25 opposite trenches 64–55 in C2 subsector. A special wire had to be laid out to observe for this to F.17.d.64. Owing to the short notice, this was not ready till 12.45pm & only 17rds were fired before 1pm. The balance of 120 were fired in the afternoon. The bombardment was repeated at the same times —	
	5/2/16	—	The left Section was withdrawn & replaced by a section of 31 LB TRFA at 7th Division. 2nd Lt S.J. Webb who has been attached for instruction was transferred to D/85 RFA who had taken up an alternative position at E.12.a.0.6.15. covering the new front for the 18th Division. The 7th Division taking over D sector of the 16th Division E sector; the 18th Division keeping 2 brigade in the line & one in reserve.	
	6/2/16	—		
	7.2.16	—	The Right Section was withdrawn. The wagon line was moved from RIBEMONT to BUIRE on the afternoon & moved to LAVIEVILLE on the night of the 5/6. A letter was received from 18th Div RA forwarding a letter from Col Blinds Cmdg 84th Bde & Centre Group calling attention to the excellent work of the battery & a memo from the O.C. 85th Bde compliments the battery on the report.	

WAR DIARY
or
INTELLIGENCE SUMMARY

Army Form C. 2118

Place	Date	Hour	Summary of Events and Information	Remarks and references to Appendices
LAVIEVILLE	2/16 1/2/16		Bty equipment overhauled & what (possible) to complete - training of specialists and drill have carried on.	
	11-29th		Much snow & frost interfering with training, only exercise possible. Watering lists to be done at BUIRE until the R.E. installed a pump in the centre of the village which pumped from a well & through accommodation in billets. The whole village having been prepared for close billets in two or three tiers of beds boards.	
			During the period the battery was in action 12-8-15 to 7-2-16 the battery fired the following:-	

A ordered 86 Shrapnel 574 H.E.
B   "   33   539 H.E.
C   "   44   524 H.E.
D   "   31   519 H.E.
          ───   ─────
          194   2156

= 2350.

W Ammatus
Capt
Cmmdg 185 RFA

WAR DIARY
or
INTELLIGENCE SUMMARY
(Erase heading not required.)

Army Form C. 2118

Place	Date	Hour	Summary of Events and Information	Remarks and references to Appendices
BURE	1.2.16		Major CARRUTHERS reconnoitred new position near NEAULTE, at E.12.a.16. Lieut JONES with gunners 2CO'd i/c advance to work on the position.	Trench Map 62d NE2 NEAULTE 1:10,000
"	2.2.16		Battery moves to NEAULTE & takes over lines from vacated by B/85.	
NEAULTE	3.2.16		T.f.	
"	4.2.16		T.f.	
"	5.2.16		Enemy balloon & aeroplanes hidden work of B, C, & D guns came into position & ranging T.f.	
"	6.2.16		Registration of zone begun. 2/Lieut TILL attached for instruction.	
"	7.2.16		Registering T.f.	
"	8.2.16		Lieut WHEELER posted to the battery. R.E. corporal attached to assist in gun pits T.f.	
"	9.2.16		Same as T.f.	
"	10.2.16		Fatigue party fetching wood got shelled by 77 mm & Sgt RING both wounded T.f.	Trench Map 57 SE 4 CUILLERS 1:10,000
"	11.2.16		Major CARRUTHERS assumes command of Right Group whilst Col BLOIS is on leave.	
"	12.2.16		Battery observes to have an F.O.O. every evening in B/141 OP at X.25.b.64 T.f.	
"	13.2.16		Same registering zone. T.f.	
"	14.2.16		T.f.	
"	15.2.16		A gun came into position & lie waving T.f.	
"	16.2.16		Same as above. am T.f.	
"	17.2.16		Same registering zone T.f.	
"	18.2.16		T.f.	
"	19.2.16		T.f.	

Army Form C. 2118

WAR DIARY
or
INTELLIGENCE SUMMARY
(Erase heading not required.)

Instructions regarding War Diaries and Intelligence Summaries are contained in F. S. Regs, Part II. and the Staff Manual respectively. Title Pages will be prepared in manuscript.

Place	Date	Hour	Summary of Events and Information	Remarks and references to Appendices
NEAULTE	20.2.16	5PM	Very clear, little wind. One enemy & German aeroplanes & observer balloon in sight. T.J.	
"	21.2.16	T.J.	12 77mm shells fell in battery posn. T.J.	
"	22.2.16	6 to 30 AM	a few 77m shells behind battery. (D3)	
"		6 PM	Got S.O.S. fire and opened an rapid rate of fire 110 rounds; about 100 77m shells fell just in front of & 58th Battery position. T.J.	
"	23.2.16		behind battery. firing barrage on track between batteries & 58th Battery position. T.J.	
"			Snapstream T.J.	
"	24.2.16		T.J.	
"	25.2.16		Heavy shins T.J. Register our left support lines. 2nd Lt TAYLOR attached to battery. T.J.	
"	26.2.16		Register our left support lines.	
"	27.2.16		T.J.	
"	28.2.16		T.J. Officers from A/96 came to see fire position T.J.	
"	29.2.16	6.45PM	Got S.O.S. D3 rapid rate of fire 104 rounds. T.J.	

[signature] Lieut. R.F.A.
for Major R.F.A.
COMMANDING D BATTERY,
96th BRIGADE. R.F.A

85 RFA
Vol 8

MAP

Army Form C. 2118

WAR DIARY
or
INTELLIGENCE SUMMARY
(Erase heading not required.)

Instructions regarding War Diaries and Intelligence Summaries are contained in F.S. Regs., Part II. and the Staff Manual respectively. Title Pages will be prepared in manuscript.

Place	Date	Hour	Summary of Events and Information	Remarks and references to Appendices
MEAULTE	1.3.16	11 AM	Capt. CALNAN of A/164 visits battery position. T.J.	
"	2.3.16		Right Section of A/164 takes over guns + gun pits in the afternoon. T.J.	
"	3.3.16		Remainder of A/164 take over Battery stores & BRESLE. Lieut JONES remains to help 9 AM onwards to assist relieving Battery. T.J.	
BRESLE	4.3.16		5 men Battery leave BRESLE 12 noon & reach BUSSY 2.30 p.m. T.J.	
BUSSY	5.3.16			
"	6.3.16		Lieut WHEELER proceeds on leave. T.J.	
"	7.3.16		T.J.	
"	8.3.16		T.J.	
"	9.3.16		Major CARROTHERS to hospital. Battery leaves BUSSY 9 A.M. & reaches La Bois des TAILLES 2.30 P.M. Left section goes on to new position near SUZANNE at A 26 d 59. Lieut GODFREY in command. T.J.	¼ Trench Map 62°NW 1 MARICOURT 1:10,000 FRANCE 62°NE Edition 2
SUZANNE	10.3.16		Battery begins making position. Right Section comes up 9pm. 2/Lt TAYLOR remains with the Negro Line at K.18.b.49 in la BOIS DES TAILLES. T.J.	
"	11.3.16		Registration of 4.3 one begun. T.J.	
"	12.3.16		German observation balloon makes registration undesirable. T.J.	
"	13.3.16		T.J.	
"	14.3.16		Some registration done. T.J.	
"	15.3.16		2/Lieut SYLVESTER temporarily attached from B3 B.A.C. T.J.	
"	16.3.16		Position for new O.P. behind LAPREE WOOD (A14 c 55.20) chosen T.J.	
"	17.3.16		8 nd metallin fuse let us burning T.J.	
"	18.3.16		T.J.	

Army Form C. 2118

WAR DIARY
or
INTELLIGENCE SUMMARY

(Erase heading not required.)

Instructions regarding War Diaries and Intelligence Summaries are contained in F.S. Regs., Part II. and the Staff Manual respectively. Title Pages will be prepared in manuscript.

Place	Date	Hour	Summary of Events and Information	Remarks and references to Appendices
SUZANNE	19.3.16		2/Lieut SYLVESTER (attached fm. B.A.C.) proceeded on leave. T.J.	
"	20.3.16		T.J.	
"	21.3.16		T.J.	
"	22.3.16		MAJOR CARRUTHERS M.V.O. D.S.O. granted sick leave. Lieut. WHEELER promoted Captain & Command of Battery from 14.3.16 – 16. T.J.	
"	23.3.16		R.E. were employed & ordered to assist in making gun pits. T.J.	
"	24.3.16		5/Lieut. CAPTAIN WHEELER returns off Carp of LARKHILL T.J.	
"	25.3.16		T.J.	
"	26.3.16		T.J.	
"	27.3.16		2/Lieut WHITBURN and 9 N.C.O.s & men of 5th Bty. 4th Home Counties Bde R.F.A (T) attached for instruction. T.J. 12 rounds rotated. 3PM. 6PM 6 howitzer rounds & 2HE 4.2 shells fell between the Battery & B/150 position T.J.	
"	28.3.16		T.J.	
"	29.3.16		Lieut GODFREY goes to hospital sick & 2/Lieut TAYLOR comes up to Battery T.J.	
"	30.3.16		9a Amn 23 HE retaliation fired. T.J.	
"	31.3.16		T.J.	

[signature]
Capt R.A.
COMMANDING D BATTERY,
86th BRIGADE, R.F.A.

Confidential

85 R.F.A. Army Form C. 2118

WAR DIARY
INTELLIGENCE SUMMARY
(Erase heading not required.)

Instructions regarding War Diaries and Intelligence Summaries are contained in F. S. Regs., Part II. and the Staff Manual respectively. Title Pages will be prepared in manuscript.

Place	Date	Hour	Summary of Events and Information	Remarks and references to Appendices
LAVIEVILLE	1.3.16		H.Q. Bde C/85 & 85 B/A.C at LAVIEVILLE	RSW
Do	2.3.16	12noon	C/85 move to BOIS des TAILLES for attachment to 30 Divn	RSW
Do	3.3.16	9.30 a.m	H.Q. Bde & Br. B.A.C. move to BUSSY LES DAOURS	RSW
BUSSY LES DAOUR	3.3.16	2pm	H.Q. & BAC arrive BUSSY LES DAOURS a small vllge 8 miles East of AMIENS. Billets appointed to each section.	RSW
Do	4.3.16	5"	A & D/85 move to BUSSY LES DAOURS	RSW
Do	7.3.16	8.30 am	A.D.V.M. — 85 BdeR.F.A move to BOIS des TAILLES for attachment to 30 Divn	RSW
Do		9 am	HQ. move to BRAY sur SOMME	RSW
BRAY	22.3.16	2pm	H.Q. arrive BRAY	RSW
BRAY	31.3.16		H.Q. A.H. @ BRAY	RSW

Rowythe
Comdg 85 Bde RFA

A/85/R27
Vol 8
MHL

WAR DIARY
or
INTELLIGENCE SUMMARY

Army Form C. 2118

A/85 R77

Place	Date	Hour	Summary of Events and Information	Remarks and references to Appendices
ALBERT	1/3/16		Fired 7 Rds BX retaliation to French Mortars in La BOISELLE. 32nd Divn Infantry relieved 17th Divn in our Sector	MWP
	2/3/16		1 Section B/164 relieved section A/85.	MWP
BRESLE	3/3/16		At 6pm B/164 (32nd Divn) relieved A/85, taking over our guns. A/85 Wagon line to BRESLE at 8.30am. Remainder of Battery to BRESLE 6pm	MWP
BUSSY	4/3/16		Battery marched at 11.30 a.m. to BUSSY LES DAOURS (5 miles E of AMIENS)	MWP
	5/3/16		On rest at BUSSY	MWP
	6/3/16		ditto	
	7/3/16		ditto	
	8/3/16		At 4.30 pm received orders to move next day to take up position at A27B 10.45. Ref MARICOURT Trench map. 62C NW1. Battery comes under orders of 30th Division	MARICOURT Trench Map 62C NW1
	9/3/16		Marched off at 8.30 am via DAOURS – CORBIE – to BOIS DES TAILLES (where the battery had its Wagon line. At 6pm the battery moved off via BRAY – CAPPY – SUZANNE to position A27B 10.45, SE of Copse D. Pits had been made by 30th Division guns and ammunition dumped in Copse D at 9.30 pm	62 DNE FRANCE 1/20,000 MWP MARICOURT Trench Map 62CNW1 MWP
MARICOURT	10/3/16		During the day work was done preparing the position. Guns placed in the pits in evening. Battery in Right Group, covers Y3 Sub sector – i.e. from MARICOURT – PERONNE ROAD to A29 Bqsqs. S.O.S lines to be registered, after which the battery to be marked & not to fire except in case of attack	MWP

Army Form C. 2118

WAR DIARY
or
INTELLIGENCE SUMMARY
(Erase heading not required.)

Instructions regarding War Diaries and Intelligence Summaries are contained in F.S. Regs., Part II. and the Staff Manual respectively. Title Pages will be prepared in manuscript.

Place	Date	Hour	Summary of Events and Information	Remarks and references to Appendices
MARICOURT	11/3/16		Work continued on position. Registered A23.B 9109 — A23.B 9100 — A23A 9340 — A23B 0030	MARICOURT TRENCH MAP 62c N.W. 1/10000
	12/3/16		— A23B 1545 for S.O.S line. 52 Rounds BX expended. Weather fine. MWP	
	13/3/16		Digging & construction. Weather very fine. MWP	
	14/3/16		Registered point A10d 85 in CENTRE GROUP. 30BX expended. MWP	
	15/3/16			
	16/3/16		Digging & construction. Weather very fine. Telephone wires laid. MWP	
	17/3/16			
	18/3/16		18th Division Infantry taking over. MWP	
	19/3/16			
	20/3/16		18th Divisional artillery relieved eastern & 30th Div Artillery Remainder 18th Div'l Artillery came in. 18th Divisional Artillery HQ took over command the	
	21/3/16			
	22/3/16		Quiet. Battery in Right Group, & to support Y.3. Sub sector. MWP	
	23/3/16			
	24/3/16		Draw Digging & timber hauling. Bdr H.Q. moved to BRAY. MWP	
	25/3/16			
	26/3/16		Digging & construction. MWP	
	27/3/16		Major TREASURE & 10 NCO's & Men from HOME COUNTIES (HOW) BDE T.F attached for instruction. MWP	

1875 Wt. W593/826 1,000,000 4/15 J.B.C. & A. A.D.S.S./Forms/C.2118.

WAR DIARY
or
INTELLIGENCE SUMMARY

(Erase heading not required.)

Army Form C. 2118

Place	Date	Hour	Summary of Events and Information	Remarks and references to Appendices
MARICOURT	28/3/16			MARICOURT TRENCH MAP 62c NW1
	29/3/16		Registered CHAPEAU DE GENDARME (A 29 D 80 85) for V2. Digging. Fine.	MAP
	30/3/16		Wire laid to CROWS NEST (MARGNY MILL) A 29 D 58 for purposes of registration.	MAP 2LIEUT AVERILL
	31/3/16		Battery Wagon Lines moved from BOIS DES TAILLES to L 20 D B 58 attached to X 18 Trench Mortar Battery for instruction.	MAP
			General	
			The zone allotted to A/85 (1 & V3) is difficult to observe, owing to the steep slopes of the Y WOOD.	
			O.Ps for the battery are as follows	
			For northern end, i.e. from PERONNE ROAD to A 23 central — O P in front line about A 23 c 58.	
			For South end of Y WOOD & front line & communication trenches running E & W, — OP CROWS NEST, an advanced infantry post on the bluff W of CHAPEAU DE GENDARME (about A 29 D 58)	
			For V2 and back part of Y 3 the OP will be constructed on road between VAUX WOOD & VAUX HANGAR (VAUX 62° NW 3)	

W Wilkes Capt
Cmdg A/85 R??

85 R 3 A
c/Batt
Vol 6

MHR

WAR DIARY or INTELLIGENCE SUMMARY

Army Form C. 2118

March 1916

Place	Date	Hour	Summary of Events and Information	Remarks and references to Appendices
LAVIEVILLE	1.3.16		On 1st March, orders were received that 55th Bde (i.e. 1/55, B.A.C. & HQ) were to march to BUSSY near AMIENS on 3.3.16. The 18th Divl Arty being withdrawn on 2/3 & 3/3 – at 11.15am on the 2nd orders were received that 1/55 was to march at 12 noon to BOIS de TAILLES & come under the orders of G.O.C. R.A. 30th Divn. – The battery arrived at BOIS de TAILLES Bois 3pm. The 30th Divn (equivalent to come into action the same evening covering the trenches South of the SOMME from FRISE E. BOISde la VACHE. The battery was in action at G 10 A 2 4 the same evening at 12.15am with all ammunition limbered with guns. The main Res/s known & only Batty preps & platforms & platforms & shell stores were available. HQ 30th Divn & ETINEHEM. J Bn Infy & Suzanne.	
2.3.16	–	Barrage lines for each gun were registered & taken over from the section of D 151 which had been covering the front.	
3-13/3/16		Continuous work at dug outs & gun positions & O.P. The first days were very wet & the dug outs flooded constantly in consequence. Very quiet in front except for German artillery activity – Telephone lines to HQ & No 2 Dn Arty (Colonel) of the head at CAPPY. The French HQ invited us over & we had much myths "aeroplane" photos. The orderly officer of the French HQ showed BC round the French trenches – The orderly officer brought the CO of the Infantry battalion to our OP to see the French front – German our bombardment of the German lines + front & were allotted for this – The 18th Divn commenced taking over from the 30th Divn – 4 & 25 were allotted for this – The 18th Divn commenced taking over from the 30th Divn –
12.3.16			
14.3.16			
19.3.16			
19-3rd		The French asked us to shell an O.P in am as were saved & only fires in case of necessity –

Army Form C. 2118

WAR DIARY
or
INTELLIGENCE SUMMARY
(Erase heading not required.)

C/65 March

Place	Date	Hour	Summary of Events and Information	Remarks and references to Appendices
	28.3.16		The mess dugout & Officers' mess & gunners' completed & the telephone dug out was completed.	
	29.3.16		Orders received that we were to dig a new position necessitating field day on 25. G10A 55·10 – our forward position G10A 10.14 being considered dangerous from gas shell – D15d which were in action alongside at G10A 2·3 are to move to G10A 0.5 –	
	30.3.16		Work commenced on new position. Material very scarce. Position on top of a 30 ft bank, the bank being covered with brushwood. A screen is being placed above the edge. A party of 11 men from the 8th Territorial Inn. Dn. Battery attached for instruction. During the month the Germans have shelled the vicinity of Bois de la VACHE daily & SUZANNE, CAPPY, VAUX frequently – shelled any likely spot near the ECOLE de VAUX which might be an O.P.	

M. Armstrong
Capt
C/65

85 R F A
Vol 9

XIII

Confidential
War Diary

of

85 Brigade R.F.A. Hd. Qrs.

from 1.4.16
to 30.4.916

Vol I

Army Form C. 2118

WAR DIARY
or
INTELLIGENCE SUMMARY

(Erase heading not required.)

Instructions regarding War Diaries and Intelligence Summaries are contained in F.S. Regs., Part II. and the Staff Manual respectively. Title Pages will be prepared in manuscript.

Place	Date	Hour	Summary of Events and Information	Remarks and references to Appendices

1875 Wt. W593/826 1,000,000 4/15 J.B.C. & A. A.D.S.S./Forms/C. 2118.

Vol 87
A/85 RFA
XVIII

WAR DIARY
or
INTELLIGENCE SUMMARY
(Erase heading not required.)

Army Form C. 2118

Instructions regarding War Diaries and Intelligence Summaries are contained in F.S. Regs., Part II. and the Staff Manual respectively. Title Pages will be prepared in manuscript.

Place	Date	Hour	Summary of Events and Information	Remarks and references to Appendices
MARICOURT	1/4/16		Registration. 15 Rounds BX. MAJOR TREASURE & detachment of KENT BTY.T.F. left. MEP	
	2/4/16		Quiet. MEP	
	3/4/16		Lieut F. ALLEN attached to the battery from Reserve Bde WOOLWICH. MEP	
	4/4/16		Registration Quiet Fine MEP	
	5/4/16		KENT BATTERY. T.F. dugout position in Copse C. under A/85 instructions MEP	
	6/4/16		Fine. Quiet. MEP	
	7/4/16			
	8/4/16			
	9/4/16		Germans shelled MARICOURT SUZANNE valley with 10·5cm shells from 6pm to midnight. MEP	
	10/4/16		Quiet. Rain. at 10pm message received stating that a prisoner captured by French South of SOMME said that Germans were going to attack on both sides of the SOMME this week. MEP Registration 21 rounds BX.	
	11/4/16		Rain. quiet. Registration 39 RX MEP	
	12/4/16		MARICOURT-SUZANNE valley shelled at 3.35pm. 24 Rounds from 150mm How. MEP	
	13/4/16	2 a.m.	Batteries in MARICOURT-SUZANNE valley shelled, & trenches in A Sector, preliminary to hostile raid. MEP	
	14/4/16		Quiet. MEP	
	15/4/16			
	16/4/16		Nothing unusual occurred MEP	
	17/4/16			
	18/4/16			

WAR DIARY or INTELLIGENCE SUMMARY

Army Form C. 2118

(Erase heading not required.)

Place	Date	Hour	Summary of Events and Information	Remarks and references to Appendices
MARICOURT	19/4/16		From 7.15 pm to 8.15pm hostile 150 mm How. Battery shelled battery at near K Copse. About 100 rounds fell of which almost 50% were blind. MaP	MARICOURT TRENCH MAP 62 C NW 1
	20/4/16		Quiet. MaP	
	21/4/16		Enemy shelled our trenches at intervals throughout the day in short bursts. We retaliated with 21BX on trench from A 23 B 0615 to A 23 B 341. Registration carried out on A 23 D 10. 35 BX fired. MaP	
	22/4/16		Quiet	
	22/4/16		In conjunction with 18 Pdrs, 4 6" Hows we fired a short burst on enemy trenches at 4.30 pm. firing 12 BX. MaP	
	23/4/16		Quiet. At 9pm fired at hostile working party at A 23 D 10, dispersing them. MaP	
	24/4/16		Enemy shelled valley in morning. Right Group batteries retaliated at 10.45 am on JIGSAW COPSE. (16 BX). At 5pm we put two salvos in German trenches in retaliation to the howitzers MaP. At night the battery moved into a position prepared at COPSE C.	
	25/4/16		From 11 a.m to 3 p.m registered points in new Zone (Z3). A9b560 - A9b472. A9b 6078 A9b78.49. At same time fired at other points to distract enemy's attention from the careful registration of the former points. Very fine a2 BX - 93 expended MaP	

Army Form C. 2118

WAR DIARY
or
INTELLIGENCE SUMMARY
(Erase heading not required.)

Place	Date	Hour	Summary of Events and Information	Remarks and references to Appendices
MARICOURT	26/4/16		From 11.45am to 2.30pm registered more points carefully, also shelling other portions of the line. 12 BX - 12 B expended.	MARICOURT TRENCH MAP 62cNW1 Very fine
	27/4/16		At 1.30am bombardment of German defences opposite A.9.2 Sub Sectors commenced, being carried out in support of two raiding parties of 54th Div. Bde. We shelled redoubt junctions of trenches at A9b 45.60 – A9b 47.72 A9b.60.78 A9b 57.57 and front trench at A9b 82.40 until 1.45am expending 120 BX. Two guns then lifted from A9b 45.60 and A9b 47.72 on to front line trench from A9b 57.57 to A9b 82.40, the remaining two remaining on their original line. At 2.15am fire ceased, having fired another 131 BX. Hostile retaliation feeble. KOEP. In evening the battery resumed its old position. KOEP.	
	28/4/16	7.40am 8.30am	18 Pdr Bty (counter battery) shelled with 150mm shells. (20) Again shelled 15 shells. Hostile aeroplane observing KOEB. 2 Lieut Allen, 1 Corporal, 3 gunners transferred to Divisional Heavy Trench Mortars.	
	29/4/16		At 10.50am and at 11.20am in conjunction with 18 Pdrs 9.6" Hows we retaliated on JIGSAW COPSE. 16BX each time. KOEP. 2 Lieut TRISKEYMS attached to B5 BAC. 2 Lieut C HENRY attached from C/85.	

1875 Wt. W593/826 1,000,000 4/15 J.B.C. & A. A.D.S.S./Forms/C.2118.

M W Daw Capt.
Comdg M85/D77.

Army Form C. 2118

C/85 RFA
vol 7

XVII

C/85 R.F.A. WAR DIARY or INTELLIGENCE SUMMARY   APRIL

(Erase heading not required.)

Instructions regarding War Diaries and Intelligence Summaries are contained in F. S. Regs., Part II. and the Staff Manual respectively. Title Pages will be prepared in manuscript.

Place	Date	Hour	Summary of Events and Information	Remarks and references to Appendices
120 MM WOOD near VAUX near SUZANNE	14.4.16	—	Alternative O.P. near VAUX school ready for use. D.kit roof C. ready for roof. Timber for the pits was cut by us in SUZANNE WOOD and splits brought up by mule cart. Lt E.C. Sylvester attached to the battery as 4th Subaltern. No firing. Weapons very quiet. The French are being shelled.	
	16.4.16	—	C. and D. made telephone & mens dug outs for Capt Daley to roof. Very little firing. The Germans on bring on them 2nd line in front of CHAPTERWOOD & have also dug a new support trench to the edge of the cliff. The French are making a 75 mm gun emplacement behind VAUX wood to enfilade the German trenches. The horses at wagon line suffered from 3 weeks in rainy exposed positions near le Bois de TAILLES, with wet weather but no rain, yet new wagon line.	
	22.4.16	—	A & B pits dug out for original O.P. infantry men can now sleep there. Trolley line laid up the slope for bringing timber & ammunition up to the guns.	
	19.4.16	—	At 4 pm on 19.4.16 during a bombardment of our trenches near CAPRNOR a 5.9 howitzer from round at the battery. The first round flew away the epaulement of C gun but did no further damage. 6 other rounds fell within 50' but no damage.	
	21.4.16	—	The 75 mm gun under Lt Brouillaise was brought up to fire 100 XI into German trenches & was removed the next night. Did the thing over again in case of emergency. A 57 mm Belgian gun was located at J.H.13 & 5.00 & shelled—	

WAR DIARY
or
INTELLIGENCE SUMMARY
(Erase heading not required.)

Army Form C. 2118

Instructions regarding War Diaries and Intelligence Summaries are contained in F.S. Regs., Part II. and the Staff Manual respectively. Title Pages will be prepared in manuscript.

Place	Date	Hour	Summary of Events and Information	Remarks and references to Appendices
ZO ZANTE 26/4/16	28.4.16		Deposits from all guns completed. Officers reconnoitring out — Commenced Timber ready for C.W.D	
	29.4.16		Orders received to change personnel with A/15 II — Guns to remain — BC visited new position	
			A/15/IBC moved F28.b.41 on 29.4.16 — G10a.14 on 30.4.16 — Right section to change	
			on night of 1/2 — LX night of 2/3 May —	
	25/26	2.30am	The French Infantry asked us to shell german support trenches while they bombed	
			the front trench with trench mortars —	
			The germans retaliating we showed more activity again in the evening —	

W. Armstrong
Capt
Cmdg C/65
RFA

Army Form C. 2118

D 85 RFA Vol 9

WAR DIARY
or
~~INTELLIGENCE SUMMARY~~
(Erase heading not required.)

XVIII

Place	Date	Hour	Summary of Events and Information	Remarks and references to Appendices
SUZANNE	1.4.16		Officers & Men of 9th How Counties Territorial Howitzer Brigade leave. P.J.	Trench Maps 62e NW3 MARICOURT 1:10,000 
	2.4.16		Some registration done. Enemy shell A26c and d with 10.5 cm hows. P.J.	
	3.4.16		2Lieut ABLEY attached for instruction to the battery. P.J.	
	4.4.16			
	5.4.16		No.4 Pit finished. No.1 pit begun. P.J.	
	6.4.16			
	7.4.16	8.20 A.M	Enemy shell G3a with 120 10.5cm & 15 cm Howitzers. P.J.	
	8.4.16		Telephone pit under construction. P.J.	
	9.4.16			
	10.4.16			
	11.4.16	7 P.M.	Heavy bombardment heard in direction of FRICOURT. P.J.	
	12.4.16	11 A.M	A few Enemy 10.5cm shell fall just behind the battery. P.J.	
	13.4.16	2 A.M.	Enemy attempt raid on A2 subsection. Battery stands to but does not fire, about 75 to 77 mm & 25 to 10.5 cm fall in and around battery. P.J.	
	14.4.16			
	15.4.16		Lieut JONES goes to Wagon Line. P.J.	
	16.4.16		Lieut GODFREY to battery from Wagon line. P.J.	
	17.4.16		2d in first retaliation to enemy shelling. A.P.I. work started on OP a dug out at A19C55 30. P.J.	
	18.4.16		2Lieut ABLEY leaves. Lieut BEARD attached for instruction. P.J.	

Army Form C. 2118

WAR DIARY
or
INTELLIGENCE SUMMARY
(Erase heading not required.)

Instructions regarding War Diaries and Intelligence Summaries are contained in F.S. Regs., Part II. and the Staff Manual respectively. Title Pages will be prepared in manuscript.

Place	Date	Hour	Summary of Events and Information	Remarks and references to Appendices
	19.4.16		30 rds fired in retaliation for being shelled by line trenches. T.J.	
	20.4.16		T.J.	
	21.4.16		T.J.	
	22.4.16		60 rds fired in retaliation for heavy shelling. T.J.	
	23.4.16		Telephone pit finished. T.J.	
	24.4.16		T.J.	
	25.4.16		Registrations done. T.J.	
	26.4.16		ditto	
	27.4.16	6.13 AM	Battery open fire on trench A9b preparatory to infantry raid. 254 rds fired. T.J.	
			Lieut GODFREY proceeds on leave. T.J.	
			Lieut JONES goes up in aeroplane.	
	28.4.16		Lieut JONES returns. 2nd Lieut TAYLOR to wagon line	
			Capt WHEELER goes up in aeroplane. T.J.	
	29.4.16		T.J.	
	30.4.16	7.40 PM	SOS A1 received. Fired 14 rds when S.O.F. orders to stop. T.J.	

[signature] Capt. R.F.A.
COMMANDING D BATTERY,
85th BRIGADE, R.F.A.

Confidential

Army Form C. 2118

WAR DIARY
or
INTELLIGENCE SUMMARY

(Erase heading not required.)

Instructions regarding War Diaries and Intelligence Summaries are contained in F. S. Regs., Part II. and the Staff Manual respectively. Title Pages will be prepared in manuscript.

Place	Date	Hour	Summary of Events and Information	Remarks and references to Appendices
BRAY Sur Somme	1.4.16		Hd Qrs 85 Bde: R.F.A. Still at BRAY	PSW
Do	26.4.16		Bombs dropped from Hostile aeroplane @ 4 am wounding one man + 7 horses (3 severely, 5 slightly)	PSW
Do	30.4.16		Hd Qr Br Bde R.F.A still @ BRAY	PSW

30.4.16

Roylee
Comdg 86e R.F.A
Comdg 85 Bde R.F.A

RFA
85 Vol. 10

Confidential

War Diary

of

85 Res. R.F.A. Hd Qr

from 1.5.16 to 31.5.16

Vol. VI

Confidential

Army Form C. 2118

WAR DIARY
or
INTELLIGENCE SUMMARY

(Erase heading not required.)

Instructions regarding War Diaries and Intelligence Summaries are contained in F.S. Regs., Part II. and the Staff Manual respectively. Title Pages will be prepared in manuscript.

Place	Date	Hour	Summary of Events and Information	Remarks and references to Appendices
BRAY Sax Corps	5.5.16	-	H.Q. 85 Bde R.F.A still at BRAY	RDW
BRAY	6.5.16	3pm	H.Q. 85 Bde R.F.A left BRAY for BOIS des TAILLES	RDW
BOIS des TAILLES	6.5.16	4pm	H.Q. 85 Bde R.F.A arrived BOIS des TAILLES where Unit were encamped under Canvas	RDW
Do	15.5.16	6am	Bde. Bomb. proceeded 6 Eng (and on leave of absence)	RDW
Do	16.5.16		85 B.A.C (Bde. Amm. Col. Horses & Vehicles) - with other B.A.C's merged into 18 D.A.C. Officers + NCOs sent to Base Details pro-tem, at ABBOEUVES	RDW
Do	24.5.16	12 noon	A/85 became D/84 - C/85 became D/82 - D/85 became D/83 Hear 85 Bde R.F.A R-formed: - 85 Bde R.F.A. same D/82 became A/85 - D/83 became B/85 D/84 became C/85 85 "Horse" Bde R.F.A therefore became an "15pdr" Bde.	RDW

Confidential

Army Form C. 2118

WAR DIARY
—or—
INTELLIGENCE SUMMARY
Page II

(Erase heading not required.)

Instructions regarding War Diaries and Intelligence Summaries are contained in F.S. Regs., Part II. and the Staff Manual respectively. Title Pages will be prepared in manuscript.

Place	Date	Hour	Summary of Events and Information	Remarks and references to Appendices
Bois des Tailles	22/5/16	6 a.m.	2/Lt. L. Haybittel (Adjutant 85" Bde RFA) left to late Command of W/18 Heavy T.M. Batt. Brigade to 18 Div. newly formed in 18 Div. Att. 2/Lt W. J. Neilson Bde. orderly officer assumed duties of Adjutant but not yet appointed	RSW
D°	26/5/16	8 a.m.	Bde. Comdt. returned from leave of absence	RSW
D°	31.11.16		HQ 85 Bde. R.F.A. 31.11.16 in Bois des Tailles	RSW

RSWoyle
Lt Col Cmdg
85" Bde R.F.A.

WAR DIARY
or
INTELLIGENCE SUMMARY

(Erase heading not required.)

Army Form C. 2118

Place	Date	Hour	Summary of Events and Information	Remarks and references to Appendices
			A/85 R.F.A.	
NORTH WEST OF BRAY.	1916 25th To 31st May.		On May 24th the Battery ceased to be D. Battery, 82nd Brigade, R.F.A. and under the scheme of reorganization became A Battery, 85th Brigade, R.F.A. In action in the NORTH embankment of the Railway loop, N.W. of BRAY near BRONFAY FARM., taken over from D/150 Brigade, R.F.A. on 22nd of March. Work done in reconstructing and strengthening position, and in building a Battle Observation Post. Very little firing during this time.	

A/85 RFA
May & June
Vol 9.16

WAR DIARY or INTELLIGENCE SUMMARY

Army Form C. 2118

(Erase heading not required.)

Place	Date	Hour	Summary of Events and Information	Remarks and references to Appendices
NORTH WEST OF BRAY	1916 June 1st to 13th		A/85 RFA. Continued to rebuild position, and construct underground control and Battle Observation Post. Most of this work was finished by the end of the first week of June.	
	13th to 24th		At 11.55 P.M. of the night of the 13th inst. received S.O.S. call and fired 474 rounds battering the enemy front line. The enemy's infantry did not leave their trenches. Constructed Ammunition recesses for 5000 rounds and got all ready for the ensuing operations. Carried out a little preliminary registration of Battle Front.	
	24th	8 A.M.	Commenced wire cutting at 8 A.M. in morning.	
	24th to 30		Cut wire, carried out concentrations on enemy trenches, and strong points. Bombarded his lines of communications and cut wire at night. Very little troubled by enemy except for some gas shells at night, which were inconvenient. We had no further harm. Wire cutting was carried out at ranges up to 3800x. The shortest range being 3300x. Wire ramps intensitated a large expenditure of shell. An examination of wire cut after the battle shewed that the fire had been sufficiently effective. The infantry experienced no difficulty in going through.	

85 RFA
vol II

Confidential

War Diary

XVIII

of

85th Brigade R.F.A. H.Qrs.

from 1.6.16 to 30.6.16

Vol VII

Confidential

Army Form C. 2118

WAR DIARY
or
INTELLIGENCE SUMMARY

(Erase heading not required.)

Instructions regarding War Diaries and Intelligence Summaries are contained in F.S. Regs., Part II. and the Staff Manual respectively. Title Pages will be prepared in manuscript.

Place	Date	Hour	Summary of Events and Information	Remarks and references to Appendices
BOIS des TAILLES	1.6.16		85" Bde: R.F.A. Hd Qrs still in the Bois des Tailles	M
do	2.6.16		H.Q. move to different site in Bois des Tailles	M
do	4.6.16		Lt Col R.D. Coyde Bde bringt to Hospital, and struck off strength of Bde.	M
do	26.6.16		Lt Col. Hope Johnstone join Brigade in Command - Knees from England	M
do	30.6.16		85" B.H.Q. still in Bois des Tailles	M

AH Hope Jnr
Lt Col R.F.A
Comdg 85" Bde R.F.A.

1875 Wt. W593/826 1,000,000 4/15 J.B.C. & A. A.D.S.S./Forms/C. 2118.

Confidential

WAR DIARY

of

85th Brigade R.F.A.

From 1.7.16 to 31.7.16

Vol. VIII

Army Form C. 2118

Confidential

WAR DIARY
or
INTELLIGENCE SUMMARY
(Erase heading not required.)

Instructions regarding War Diaries and Intelligence Summaries are contained in F.S. Regs., Part II. and the Staff Manual respectively. Title Pages will be prepared in manuscript.

Place	Date	Hour	Summary of Events and Information	Remarks and references to Appendices
Bois des Tailles	1.7.16		24.9.85 Brigade RFA S/14 in to 180 des Tailles	MH
do	2.7.16		2/Lt W.H. Howe joined Brigade as adjutant on probation	MH
-"-	5-7-16	7 pm	B/85 came out of action with damaged guns of his own, & collected from other batteries.	MH
-"-	9-7-16	3-30 AM	C/85 came out of action with more damaged guns at 3-30 am.	MH
		5-30 AM	A/85 " " " " " " ", but with only 3 deal sights, having been ordered to hand one over to A/84.	
		9 am	B/85 Guns sent to I.O.M. workshop XIII Corps for overhaul.	
-"-	10-7-16		A/85 & C/85 Guns sent to I.O.M. XIII Corps workshops for overhaul. All horses arrived in poor condition & overworked.	MH
-"-	11-7-16		G.O.C. R.A. inspected the Brigade lines and was not satisfied with remounts sent as reinforcements from D.A.C. It is reported by Officers sent to XIII workshops, that the guns are being repaired by old springs being bounced, as there are not enough new springs.	MH

Confidential

Army Form. C. 2118

WAR DIARY
INTELLIGENCE SUMMARY

(Erase heading not required.)

Instructions regarding War Diaries and Intelligence Summaries are contained in F.S. Regs, Part II. and the Staff Manual respectively. Title Pages will be prepared in manuscript.

Place	Date	Hour	Summary of Events and Information	Remarks and references to Appendices
Bois de Tailles	12-7-16		O.C. Brigade went to J.O.M. XIII Corps to investigate the repair of guns. J.O.M. stated that only half the springs replaced who new, and that the other half had to be trundled. Question of a 4th technical wagon for this Brigade raised with A.D.O.S. XIII Corps.	MH
N. of Billon Wood	17-7-16		On the morning of July 17th the brigade went into action just N of FAVIERE WOOD, with the object of cutting wire on German second line immediately S.E. of GUILLEMONT, which was the extreme right of the British objective. The Germans held most of the high ground and no observation was possible. Wire was cut on the afternoon.	MH
-do-	18-7-16		Wire was cut on the morning. Germans evidently expected an attack as a continual barrage was maintained with 15 c.m.f, 10.5 c.m and 77 m guns & howitzers on our support trenches and approaches. Owing to delay in attack rôle of 85th Bde. developed into harassing the exits from GUILLEMONT on the occasion of various English and French attacks and German counter attacks. Capt Trumplin attached to Brigade & took over command of A/85 " " " C/85 Think Paterson	MH
-do-	19-7-16		Under orders of G.O.C. 30 Divisional Artillery. Wire cutting was suspended, & the time employed in improving battery position. The German first line was about 900' from the Batteries, that the Germans advanced 100 yds on the high ground by Malty HORN FARM (SW of GUILLEMONT) they could there had the 15th Bde & 148 Bde under direct observation. As it was on an average probably about 300. 15 cm shells, 300 of 10.5 cm, & about 200. 77 mm shells fell daily within 250 yds of the two Brigades & caused practically no damage to equipment or Personnel.	MH

Army Form C. 2118

WAR DIARY
or
INTELLIGENCE SUMMARY
(Erase heading not required.)

Confidential

Instructions regarding War Diaries and Intelligence Summaries are contained in F.S. Regs., Part II. and the Staff Manual respectively. Title Pages will be prepared in manuscript.

Place	Date	Hour	Summary of Events and Information	Remarks and references to Appendices
N of Billon Wood	20/7/16	3 a.m.	One section of each Battery withdrawn to Billon Wood, handing over guns complete to sections of 157th Bde. 35th Divl Art.	M.H.
		9 p.m.	Remaining sections of each Battery withdrawn to Billon Wood, handing over guns complete to section of 157 Bde. 35th Divl Art. 2/Lt S.T. Rees joined Bde from 2/Lt S.T. Rees } joined Bde from 157th Bde." 3 January 15 S.A.C. New guns were taken over to complete from 157th Bde.	M.H.
Billon Wood	21-7-16	9.30 a.m.	The Bde marched from BILLON WOOD to N. BOIS DE TAILLES. Under orders of 18th Divl Art. Handed over 7 guns complete without sights, & 3 guns complete with sights to 82nd Bde. Received from 52nd Bde R.F.A. 3 guns with one dial sight, & 1 gun from 30th Divn stripped.	M.H.
Northern Bois de Tailles	22-7-16	1-30 p.m.	Proceeded on Route March to QUERRIEU, & went into Bivouac. Received from 30M 13th Corps, Corbie, 5 Guns stripped (one of which was unrepaired) also 1 unrepaired 18 Pr Ammn. Wagon.	M.H.
Querrieu	23-7-16	8 a.m.	Marched to ALLERY & went into Billets	M.H.
ALLERY	24/7/16		Detailed examination of guns & stores carried out.	M.H.
ALLERY	27/7/16		Bde marched from ALLERY to LONGPRÉ & entrained for BAILLEUL, & then marched to EECKE & CAESTRE arriving there about 2 a.m. 28-7-16	M.H.
CAESTRE	28/7/16		Bde Hd Qrs went into Billets at CAESTRE, & Batteries at EECKE	

P.W. Hoare Lt Col R.A. Lieut Col.
Comdg 85th Brigade, Royal Field Artillery

Confidential

War Diary

of

3rd Infantry Bde

from 1.8.16

31.8.16

Vol IX

Army Form C. 2118

Confidential

WAR DIARY
or
INTELLIGENCE SUMMARY

(Erase heading not required.)

Instructions regarding War Diaries and Intelligence Summaries are contained in F.S. Regs., Part II. and the Staff Manual respectively. Title Pages will be prepared in manuscript.

Place	Date	Hour	Summary of Events and Information	Remarks and references to Appendices
EECKE & CAESTRE	1-8-16	10 a.m.	Preliminary Reconnaissance of Battery Positions at BOIS GRENIER by Bde. Commanders.	NAH
-do-	2-8-16	6 p.m.	Bde. marched from EECKE to CROIX DU BAC. into Preliminary Position. Hd Qrs into Battle Hqrs at H 17 d. 35. 40. Bde is supporting the 7th E. Surrey Regt.	NAH
South of BOIS GRENIER	3-8-16		A/85 Bty Comd't reconnoitred new position, as the range was too long from Hqrs position originally selected. B/85 at work in slewing pits from which former occupants had fired in different directions. C/85 Registered with guns of 42nd Bty NEW ZEALAND Artillery into the position he was going to relieve. The Bde Hd Qrs position although at some time had been occupied before, had been vacant for some time & require rewiring to Batteries and Hqrs Brigade	NAH
-do-	4-8-16	9 p.m.	1 Section of B/85 came into action. 3 Howitzers of D/94 allotted to this Brigade	NAH
		9 p.m.	C/85 came into action in present position in row of Houses at H 26 b.3.9. OR 13 P 57	NAH
-do-	5-8-16	9 p.m.	2nd Section of B/85 came into action & completed relief.	NAH
do	6-8-16	9 p.m.	2/Lt Dudley Fletcher admitted to Hospital. Continued reconnoitring for O.Ps., improving Gun Pits, & further registration carried out. A/85 came into action	NAH

1875 Wt. W593/826 1,000,000 4/15 J.B.C. & A. A.D.S.S./Forms/C. 2118.

Army Form C. 2118

WAR DIARY
or
INTELLIGENCE SUMMARY

(Erase heading not required.)

Confidential

Instructions regarding War Diaries and Intelligence Summaries are contained in F.S. Regs., Part II. and the Staff Manual respectively. Title Pages will be prepared in manuscript.

Place	Date	Hour	Summary of Events and Information	Remarks and references to Appendices
South of BOIS GRENIER	7-8-16	1 am	Enemy attempted to carry out a raid, on that of front defended by E SURREY Regt. after heavy bombardment by guns & trench Mortars. S.O.S barrage was put up, assistance being given by F & Bde R.F.A. Work continued on Pits, O.P's. & further Registration carried out.	MHH
- Do -	8-8-16		Continuation of work on Gun Pits, O.Ps, & registration	MHH
- Do -	9-8-16	11 am	About 200 . 4.2 shells dropped near BRIS POT assisted by enemy aeroplane observation. Damage Nil.	MHH
		9 pm	The 7th E.Yorks (the Buffs)Bde. relieved the 7th E.Surreys Regt.	
- Do -	11-8-16	4 pm	2nd Lt F.N.W BROWN Joined from D.A.C. & attached to B/85. Registration by aid of Aeroplane observation carried out by B/85 & D/84. Work continued on Gun Pits & O.Ps.	MHH
- Do -	12-8-16	11 am	Retaliation carried out on Enemys support trenches in reply to enemy shelling of our front line (Trench 51). Enemy stopped shelling. Reconnoitring for alternative Gun Positions	MHH
Do	13-8-16	6.50 pm	Work continued on Pits & O.Ps. Retaliation carried out on Enemys front & support trenches opposite trenches 51 & 52. Enemy stopped shelling	MHH MHH
	14-8-16	3.45 4.20 6.30	Retaliation carried out in reply to enemy shelling BOIS GRENIER. Enemy stopped shelling.	MHH

Confidential

Army Form C. 2118

WAR DIARY
or
INTELLIGENCE SUMMARY
(Erase heading not required.)

Instructions regarding War Diaries and Intelligence Summaries are contained in F. S. Regs., Part II. and the Staff Manual respectively. Title Pages will be prepared in manuscript.

Place	Date	Hour	Summary of Events and Information	Remarks and references to Appendices
South of BOIS GRENIER	15 & 16/8/16		Work continued on Pits. O.P. & Screens.	APH
-do-	17/8/16	3.45	Retaliation carried out in reply to enemy shelling BOIS GRENIER, enemy stopped shelling	APH
-do-	18/8/16	9-15 9-35	" " " " Pat. Trap. Enemy stopped shelling " " " " Pits. O.P. & Screens. A/85 Gun Pits completed. Probably S.9 pts.	APH APH
-do-	19/8/16	2 pm	Owing to the quietness of the enemy, an agressive scheme was employed.	APH
-do-	20/8/16	1 pm 2-15 pm 2.30 pm	Each O. Officer of A, B & C Batteries of 53rd Bde reported at various times between 1pm & 2-15 pm that enemy were shelling trenches 47 & 48, also Bn Hd Qrs Brick City. The O.C. 7th Buffs was notified in each case, but requested that no retaliation be carried out. The O.C. 7th Buffs Regt asked for retaliation, which was duly carried out at 2.50 pm & again at 3. 8 pm.	APH
-do-	21/8/16		Lt Crouch A/85 admitted to Hospital. O.C. 7th Buffs changed Bn. Hd. Qrs from White City to Moat Farm. Telephone wires had to be relaid.	APH
	23/8/16		Bde & Bty Commanders of 152 Bde RFA 34th Div. Schen hend previous to taking over. One Officer per Bde proceeded to TINGUES to procure billets in new area.	APH

Confidential

Army Form C. 2118

WAR DIARY
or
INTELLIGENCE SUMMARY
(Erase heading not required.)

Instructions regarding War Diaries and Intelligence Summaries are contained in F.S. Regs., Part II. and the Staff Manual respectively. Title Pages will be prepared in manuscript.

Place	Date	Hour	Summary of Events and Information	Remarks and references to Appendices
South of BOIS GRENIER	24/5/16	9.05pm	1st section B/95 relieved } by sections of 152 Bde R.F.a.	MH
		10.10pm	" A/55 "	MH
		10.2pm	" C/55 "	
			All wires and circuits trench handed over to 152 Bde R.F.A.	
	25/5/16	7am	Registration carried out by relieving sections 152 Bde R.F.A.	MH
			One section per Battery with remaining wagons marched to concentration area at G.3.C.1.9. Map reference Trones Sheet 36 NW.	
		9.30pm	2nd section relieved & marched to concentration area.	
		11pm	Command of section handed over to 152 Bde R.F.A.	
N.W. of CROIX du BAC	27/5/16	10am	Bde Comdt attends conference of L.O.C. R.A. at BAILLEUL	MH
-do-	29/5/16	6.15	Bde marched from CROIX du BAC to BAILLEUL & MERVILLE entrained for DOULLENS detrained at DOULLENS and AUTHIEULE & went into bivouac at AUTHIEULE	MH
AUTHIEULE	30/5/16	1pm	Bde marched from AUTHIEULE to VADENCOURT into bivouac.	MH
VADENCOURT	31/5/16	2pm	Bde marched from VADENCOURT to BRICKFIELDS Area 7 mile NW of ALBERT. Discipline of Brigade very good.	MH

McKnew Lieut & Adjt

Confidential

War Diary
of
65 Brigade — R.F.A.
18 Artly

From 1.9.16   To 30.9.16

Vol X

Vol 14

Confidential

Army Form C. 2118

WAR DIARY
or
INTELLIGENCE SUMMARY

(Erase heading not required.)

Instructions regarding War Diaries and Intelligence Summaries are contained in F. S. Regs., Part II. and the Staff Manual respectively. Title Pages will be prepared in manuscript.

Place	Date	Hour	Summary of Events and Information	Remarks and references to Appendices
Brickfields ½ mile NW Albert	1-2/7/16	9 am	Bde & Battery Commanders reconnoitred positions prior to taking over from 22nd Australian Bde R.F.A.	AWH
- do -	3/7/16	9 am	Bde Hd'qrs staff & Officer per Battery reconnoitred system of telephone communication.	AWH
		12 noon	1st section of 85th Bde relieved 1st section 22nd Australian Bde R.F.A.	
Contalmaison	4/7/10	7 am	Bde Hd'qrs and 2nd section of 85th Bde marched from Albert to Contalmaison & completed relief by 10 am. Rt.E.Mews C/85 posted to B/85; 2Lt. Brown posted from B/85 to C/85. 85th Bde supporting the Right Battn. 3rd Canadian Inf. Bde. & covering front R.34.d.7.6. to R.28.d.4.7. Map reference France 57.d SE 1/20000.	AWH
- do -	5/7/10	3.40 pm & 7 pm	Retaliation was carried out at these hours owing to Heavy shelling of front line. Normal Barrage maintained remainder of day. Telephone communication reestablished as lines taken over from 22nd Australian Bde. very unsatisfactory.	AWH
- do -	6/7/10	3.15 am & 8 pm	Retaliation was carried out at these hours, in reply to enemy heavy shelling front line. Positions bombarded intermittently during the day.	AWH

Confidential

WAR DIARY
or
INTELLIGENCE SUMMARY

Army Form C. 2118

(Erase heading not required.)

Instructions regarding War Diaries and Intelligence Summaries are contained in F. S. Regs., Part II. and the Staff Manual respectively. Title Pages will be prepared in manuscript.

Place	Date	Hour	Summary of Events and Information	Remarks and references to Appendices
Bolahmaiser	7/9/16	1-5am to 1-30am	3 S.O.S rockets observed at 1-5am, apparently sent up by left company 13th Bn. Canadian Infy. S.O.S barrage immediately turned on.	MAH
		7am to 8-20am	Retaliation carried out on enemy front line in reply to heavy shelling of support line. Remainder of day normal	MAH
"	8/9/16		Enemy aeroplanes active during day. Prairies bombarded	MAH
"	9/9/16	4-45pm	85th Bde switched on new front - (R.35.d.6.3 to 6.a.16.70) (Map Ref - Courcelette 1/5000) to take part in 18th Div Ant operation Under no. II. This operation was successfully carried out. Enemy retaliated by heavily shelling front line & support line 9 Bn Hd Qrs, but no counter attack was attempted.	MAH
"	10/9/16	3am to 6am	Prairies Heavily shelled during these hours. Battery positions also Hd Qrs were shelled, but no damage done. 85th Bde were ordered to remain on new front R.35.d.35.70 to R.35.d.95.55. Map Ref Courcelette 1/5000.	MAH
		9pm	19th Canadian Bn. 4th Bde. came into line on front covered by 85th Bde.	
"	11/9/16		2Lt R F Rowbotham joined from D.A.C & Posted to A/85 ; 2Lt E A F Campbell posted to 83rd Bde R.F.A 2Lt E J PEARSON " B/85 Lt E MEWS B/85 evacuated sick to C.C Station, 1st Canadian Divn. Normal barrage maintained during day	MAH

Confidential

Army Form C. 2118

WAR DIARY
or
INTELLIGENCE SUMMARY

(Erase heading not required.)

Instructions regarding War Diaries and Intelligence Summaries are contained in F.S. Regs., Part II. and the Staff Manual respectively. Title Pages will be prepared in manuscript.

Place	Date	Hour	Summary of Events and Information	Remarks and references to Appendices
Contalmaison	12/9/16	1.40pm	Retaliation carried out on enemy's front line & support trenches. Normal barrage maintained during remainder of day.	MH
"	13/9/16	2.47am	Retaliation carried out on enemy's front line for 15 minutes	
		11 am	Trench running from R.36.c.5.5. to R.36.c.1.7 was bombarded from 11 am to 11.30am. Map Ref. Courcelette 5000. Normal barrage during remainder of day	MH
"	14/9/16		Normal barrage maintained during day. Retaliation carried out on enemy's front line. In view of communication being maintained during operations to be carried out on the 15th inst., telephone wires were duplicated & tradded, and additional testing station manned.	MH
"	15/9/16	6.20am	18th Div 1st Operation Order No 12 commenced. 18th Div supporting the 2nd Canadian Div. taking part in the attack in conjunction with the 4th and French Armies. 15th Division on Right Flank & 3rd Canadian divn on Left Flank.	
		7.15am	Objective reported successfully gained and infantry consolidated at 7.45 am. 4550 Rds expended by Bde during attack up to 8.55 am.	MH
		9.20am	Barrage raised 300 yds over Gun Pit Road. Tanks employed for 1st time.	
		12.10pm	Rate of fire dropped to 1 Rd Per Gun Per 5 minutes.	
		1.55pm	Enemy retaliated by heavy shelling	

Confidential

WAR DIARY
or
INTELLIGENCE SUMMARY
(Erase heading not required.)

Army Form C. 2118

Instructions regarding War Diaries and Intelligence Summaries are contained in F.S. Regs., Part II. and the Staff Manual respectively. Title Pages will be prepared in manuscript.

Place	Date	Hour	Summary of Events and Information	Remarks and references to Appendices
Contalmaison	15/9/16	6 pm	18th Divn Art. Operation Order No 13 commenced. 85th Bde taking part in the support of 5th Canadian Inf/ Bde in attacking COURCELLETTE. This was successfully accomplished & COURCELLETTE was captured.	MPH
		9 pm	8 Guns of B & C Batteries were reported out of action, through spring trouble, & faulty pistons. A/85 was distributed over Bde front & maintained barrage of 50 rds per hour during night on new front (M. 26.a.4.9. to M.19.d.10.62) Map Ref 57 c SW France	MPH
"—	16/9/16	3 am	B & C Batteries came out of action to Wagon Lines. Guns were shipped & damaged springs, pistons etc were sent to 10th workshops VARENNES for repair. Gun No 384 B/85 condemned. Normal barrage maintained on new front.	MPH
"—	17/9/16	7 pm to 7.55 pm	Barrage increased to 2 Rds Per Gun Per Minute until 7.25 pm then gradually dropped to normal barrage. New Positions were reconnoitred & selected as under: A/85 x 5.c. 8.2. B/85 x 5.d. 5.8 C/85 x 5.d. 35.90 } Map Ref France 57 d SE.	MPH

Army Form C. 2118

Confidential

WAR DIARY
or
INTELLIGENCE SUMMARY
(Erase heading not required.)

Instructions regarding War Diaries and Intelligence Summaries are contained in F.S. Regs., Part II. and the Staff Manual respectively. Title Pages will be prepared in manuscript.

Place	Date	Hour	Summary of Events and Information	Remarks and references to Appendices
Contalmaison	18/9/16	6.30am	A/85 occupied new position at X 5 c 8 2. & supporting 4th Bn 1st Canadian Infy Bde.	MPH
		4.35pm	Enemy heavily shelled Contalmaison & blew up a Gun Pit of B/85. destroying a few gun stores & ammunition. Lieut T. O'Connor A.V.C attached 85th Bde evacuated sick to No #7 Field Ambulance	MPH
	19/9/16		Work continued on improving new Gun Positions. Normal Barrage maintained during day.	MPH
		9.30pm to 10.40pm	S O S Barrage.	
"	20/9/16	3.50am	S.O.S barrage maintained till 4.30 am. Front now covered by A/85 (M, 26, a, 4. 9. to M.19.d 10.62.) Map Ref. 57.C. S.W. France work continued on Gun Positions	MPH
"	21/9/16	12.40am 3.30am 4.41am	S.O.S barrage maintained till 1.15 am } Remainder of day quiet " " " 4.15 am } " " " 5.20 am } work continued on Gun Positions	MPH
"	22/9/10	3.30pm 7.30pm to 10.30pm 8.30/16 9.10pm	Enemy shelled Contalmaison to 5pm about 1 Rd per minute. France Operation Order No 19 commenced, on front (M. 25.d. 8.5 to M.25.b.8.4) Map Ref. 57.C. SW. 1 Rd Per Gun Per Minute, Rate then reduced to normal barrage at 9.50pm. Infantry report objective gained	MPH

1875 Wt. W593/826 1,000,000 4/15 J.B.C. & A. A.D.S.S./Forms/C. 2118.

Confidential

Army Form C. 2118

WAR DIARY
or
INTELLIGENCE SUMMARY

(Erase heading not required.)

Instructions regarding War Diaries and Intelligence Summaries are contained in F.S. Regs., Part II. and the Staff Manual respectively. Title Pages will be prepared in manuscript.

Place	Date	Hour	Summary of Events and Information	Remarks and references to Appendices
Contalmaison	23/9/16		Zone allotted to Bde M 26 a 3.8 to M. 20. C. 2.3. Map Ref Le SARS' 1/10000	MH
		4/7pm	C/85 came into action at X 5 d 35.90. (Map Ref Ovillers 1/10000)	
		6pm	B/85 " " " X 5 d 5.8 (" " ")	
	24/9/16	2pm	B + C Batteries registered on Barrage Zone.	MH
		6.25pm to 6.30pm	Retaliation carried out on Enemy's front line	
		10pm	6th Canadian Infy Bde relieved 1st Canadian Infy Bde on front (M 25. 70. 55. to M 19. d 0 3). 85th Bde supporting 29th Bde.	
	25/9/16		Normal Barrage maintained during day.	MH
		9.20 to 10.40	Bursts of fire on enemy troops massing in M 19 & 20 (Map Ref Le SARS)	
	26/9/16	12.35pm	Operation Order No 18 commenced. 85th Bde supporting the 29th Bn 6th Canadian Infy Bde. Objective was gained at 1-35pm.	MH
		4.53pm	Enemy reported holding trench very thick from Twenty Rd to Bapaume Rd M 19. d. 1. 9. to M 26 a 4.1, also warm as machine Gun at end of Twenty Rd M 20 c 0.3. C/85 fired at M 20 c 03 for 15 minutes + dispersed enemy who were caught by fire from A/85 + B/85 respectively causing considerable casualties. This incident was observed + reported by Liason Officer 28th Bn 6th Canadian Infy Bde.	

Confidential

WAR DIARY
or
INTELLIGENCE SUMMARY
(Erase heading not required.)

Army Form C. 2118.

Instructions regarding War Diaries and Intelligence Summaries are contained in F.S. Regs., Part II. and the Staff Manual respectively. Title Pages will be prepared in manuscript.

Place	Date	Hour	Summary of Events and Information	Remarks and references to Appendices
Coulonvilliers	26/9/16	9 p.m. to 9.30 p.m.	The town of Pys was bombarded for 30 minutes at rate of 1 Rd per gun per 2 minutes.	MWH
"	27/9/16		THIEPVAL captured by 2nd Corps.	MWH
		12.30am to 12.30 3.30pm	SOS barrage maintained.	
		7 p.m.	28th Cav. Divn. Bde are up to Bapaume Rd & in touch with 23rd Division on right. Enemy reported retiring towards LE SARS, and Patrols were sent out to clear up the situation. Barrage front allotted to Bde M15C00 to M14d00. Map Ref: Courcellette 1/5000.	MWH
		11.15	The town of Pys bombarded by HE for 5 minutes.	
--"--	28/9/16	9 p.m.	Owing to enemy wiring barrage front continually changed till 12 noon from then Bde were allotted front M15a99 B-M14 B-d.9 (Map Ref. Courcellette) 1/5000. 4th Cav. Divn. left, Bde. relieved 6th Canadian Inf. Bde.	MWH
	29/9/16	2 p.m.	Battery Cmdrs reconnoitred Positions they were to take up in front of Authuille Wood, AVE LUY WOOD, and MESNIL in 2nd Corps area in support of 18th Divn Inf. Y.	MWH
		5 p.m.	1st section of A.B.C. Batteries came out of action to wagon lines. The detachments took over guns at the following Positions same evening at 9 p.m.	

Confidential

Army Form C. 2118

WAR DIARY
or
INTELLIGENCE SUMMARY
(Erase heading not required.)

Instructions regarding War Diaries and Intelligence Summaries are contained in F. S. Regs., Part II. and the Staff Manual respectively. Title Pages will be prepared in manuscript.

Place	Date	Hour	Summary of Events and Information	Remarks and references to Appendices
Contalmaison	30/9/16	12 noon	Bde Hd 85 & remaining Sections of Batteries came out of action from X 5 c & D (Map Ref LE SARS) and took over positions from 241 Bde R.F.A. at— A/85 = W 6 d 3.6 ; B/85 W 28 d 4.44 ; C/85, W 35 d 6.6; A & C Batteries changed guns with 241 Bde R.F.A. Bde Hd & 85 remained at Wagon lines at BECOURT WOOD as Batteries took over positions which were grouped in 49th Division.	MH

W Afforde Lt & Adjt
for O.C. 85 Bde R.F.A.

1875 Wt. W593/826 1,000,000 4/15 J.B.C. & A. A.D.S.S./Forms/C. 2118.

Vol 15

Copy of his
War Diary

of

85th Brigade R.F.A.

From 1.10.16 to 31.10.16

Vol XI

Confidential

WAR DIARY
or
INTELLIGENCE SUMMARY
(Erase heading not required.)

Army Form C. 2118

Instructions regarding War Diaries and Intelligence Summaries are contained in F.S. Regs., Part II. and the Staff Manual respectively. Title Pages will be prepared in manuscript.

Place	Date	Hour	Summary of Events and Information	Remarks and references to Appendices
Beaucourt Wood.	1. 10/16		Bde. Hd. Qrs at Wagon line X.25.c.1.3 Map Ref. 57.d. S.E France. Batteries in action under Group Control of 49th Divn Art.	MHH
AUTHUILLE Wood.	2. 10/16	11.50 am	Bde Hd Qrs moved to W.12.a.4.8 (Blighty Valley) Map Ref 57A SE France. Batteries were however ordered to remain under Group Control 49th Divn. It difficulty found to establish telephone communication to Batteries, as they are spread over a wide area.	MHH
-Do-	3. 10/16		Lieut S.J. COTTON (A.V.C) Posted to 85th Bde as Veterinary Officer. Bde Commdt took over control of Batteries in their present positions. 85th Bde supporting by enfilading (Map Ref BEAUMONT. 10000) Barrage front allotted = R.19 Central to R.19.6. S.P.00. Night firing on all approaches in area between GRANDCOURT and SOS barrage zone.	MHH
-Do-	4. 10/16		Normal Barrage maintained during day + night.	MHH
-Do-	5. 10/16	7.30 am	Bombing operation commenced on Northern Portion of SCHWABEN REDOUBT. 85th Bde supporting by enfilading the HANZA LINE from R.19.6.6.4. to R.14.C.05.15. (Map Ref BEAUMONT 10000.) Bombers reached R.19.d 30.75 + R.19.C.9.9. Situation Normal.	MHH
		9 pm	7th R.W. Kent's Bn relieved by 16th Rifle Bde. 39th Divn.	

Confidential

Army Form C. 2118

WAR DIARY
or
INTELLIGENCE SUMMARY
(Erase heading not required.)

Instructions regarding War Diaries and Intelligence Summaries are contained in F. S. Regs., Part II. and the Staff Manual respectively. Title Pages will be prepared in manuscript.

Place	Date	Hour	Summary of Events and Information	Remarks and references to Appendices
AUTHUILLE WOOD	6/10/16	8 am	51st Divn Art. being withdrawn from the line the barrage front was redistributed from R.19.c.5.7. to 8.24.b.05.20. (Map Ref Beaumont 1/10000)	MH
		9 am	Battery wagon lines moved to W.16.b.25. (near AVELUY.)	
		5 pm	B/85 occupied new position at 8.27.b.95.90 and registered same day	MH
	6pm–7/10/16	6.15 pm	S.O.S. barrage commenced. Situation normal at 7.15 pm. Normal barrage maintained remainder of day.	MH
-do-	8/10/16	11 am	A/85 occupied new position at 8.22.c.05.55. (Map Ref Beaumont 1/10000)	MH
			D/85 " " " " " 8.22.c.5.0 (" " ")	
		4 pm	Bde Hd Qrs occupied new position at 8.26.d.2.2. (Mt MESNIL) –D– Normal barrage maintained during day.	
MESNIL	9/10/16	4.30 am	18th Divn Art Operation Order 23 commenced. Objective SCHWABEN REDOUBT. 85th Bde. are supporting the attack by enfilading STUFF TRENCH from R.20.a.5.1. to R.20.b.5. (Map Ref BEAUMONT 1/10000)	MH
		12.35 pm	18th Divn Art Operation Order 22 commenced. Objective STUFF REDOUBT & line R.21.a.80.12 – R.20.b.90–15. 75th Bde supporting the attack by enfilading STUFF TRENCH	MH
		2 pm	Objective reported gained. C/85 came out of action & occupied new position at 8.24.d.45 but could not register same day owing to bad visibility	MH

Army Form C. 2118

Confidential

WAR DIARY
or
INTELLIGENCE SUMMARY
(Erase heading not required.)

Instructions regarding War Diaries and Intelligence Summaries are contained in F.S. Regs., Part II. and the Staff Manual respectively. Title Pages will be prepared in manuscript.

Place	Date	Hour	Summary of Events and Information	Remarks and references to Appendices
MESNIL	9/10/16	6.10 p.m.	S.O.S Barrage maintained till 6.25 p.m. Wireless Mast installed at Bde. H.Q. 87F	MKH
-do-	10/10/16	9.30 a.m.	C/85 Registered in new Position. Normal Barrage maintained during day. 118th Infy Bde relieved the 117 Infy Bde in the line. 85th Bde supporting the 6th Cheshire Btn.	MKH
-do-	11/10/16		Normal Barrage maintained during day.	MKH
-do-	12/10/16		Gun Platforms improved & trails secured ready to cut wire on the morning of 13th. Battery hagon lines moved to W.9.c.6.6. (Map Ref. France 57d SE 1/20000)	MKH
-do-	13/10/16	9 a.m.	Wire cutting operation commenced on wire from R.19.d.30.65 to R.19.d.05.95. (Map Ref. BEAUMONT 1/10000). This was successfully cut by 12 noon same day. Infy machine guns & fixed rifles were kept on these wires during hours of darkness from 7p.m. to 11.30 p.m. & 2.30 am till dawn next day. Infy Patrols report wire completely destroyed. Operation Order 24 Postponed.	MKH

Army Form C. 2118

WAR DIARY
or
INTELLIGENCE SUMMARY
(Erase heading not required.)

Place	Date	Hour	Summary of Events and Information	Remarks and references to Appendices
MESNIL	14/10/16	2.46 pm	Operation Order No. 24 commenced. Objective, to complete the capture of SCHWABEN REDOUBT and line R.20.c.2.7 - R.19.d.9.9 - 6.9 - 4.9 - 3.9 - 1.9 - 85th Bde supporting attack by enfilading STUFF TRENCH - LUCKY WAY. The operation was successful & ahead of objective captured.	NAH
		3.40pm to 4pm	2 wireless balls were received of enemy's guns in action. These were engaged by C/85, during operations. Enemy put up heavy barrage during the operation, which slackened down considerably about 4.55pm. 85th Bde remained on STUFF TRENCH & LUCKY WAY for purposes of S.O.S. Barrage, night firing being carried out on the approaches to the Barrage line.	
-do-	15/10/16		Lieut H Godsal evacuated sick to C.C. Station from 136 Field Ambulance.	NAH
		5.30pm	Enemy heavily bombarded front line trenches, especially SCHWABEN REDOUBT.	
		9 pm	Enemy lifted their Barrage & counter-attacked on the line R.19.6.9.6 - 6.4 - 6.1 -. The S.O.S. call was taken up immediately which completely stopped the enemy's infantry.	
		10.30pm	The enemy attempted a 2nd Counter-attack, this attack being also broken up by artillery fire. German casualties were very heavy.	

Confidential

Army Form C. 2118

WAR DIARY
or
INTELLIGENCE SUMMARY
(Erase heading not required.)

Instructions regarding War Diaries and Intelligence Summaries are contained in F.S. Regs., Part II. and the Staff Manual respectively. Title Pages will be prepared in manuscript.

Place	Date	Hour	Summary of Events and Information	Remarks and references to Appendices
MESNIL	16/10/16		Normal Barrage maintained during day. 114th Infy Bde relieved 118th Bde. The 16th NOTTS & DERBYS Btn covering front R19c25 to Pivi Aucre. (Map Ref Beaumont 10000)	MH
"	17/10/16	11am	A Metallic telephone communication established from Bde Hd Qts to R.20.c.2.7 in order to carry out registration on LUCKY WAY – STUFF TRENCH – and HANZA LINE Also country in vicinity of these Points. This was successfully carried & line rolled up.	MH
		12 NOON	85th Bde R.F.A. Barrage front for S.O.S purposes were redistributed as follows:– "R19 a.6.3. to the River Aucre" (Map Ref Beaumont 10000.)	
"	18/10/16		Normal barrage maintained during day. Enemy artillery active between the hours of 5pm & 11.30pm in consequence of which all Supplies of Ammunition were ordered to be delivered to Line Units before 4pm daily.	MH
"	19/10/16		Operation order to 26 Published & returns. Normal Barrage Maintained.	MH
"	20/10/16	6am to 7am	S O S call received owing to enemy bombing the SCHWABEN REDOUBT. situation normal.	MH
		10pm	2Lt R W FAGAN evacuated sick to 3rd Fd Ambulance 63rd R.N. Divn.	MH

Confidential

WAR DIARY
or
INTELLIGENCE SUMMARY
(Erase heading not required.)

Army Form C. 2118

Instructions regarding War Diaries and Intelligence Summaries are contained in F. S. Regs., Part II. and the Staff Manual respectively. Title Pages will be prepared in manuscript.

Place	Date	Hour	Summary of Events and Information	Remarks and references to Appendices
MESNIL	21/10/16	4.55am	A slow barrage was put up owing to enemy shelling SCHWABEN REDOUBT	MPH
		5-10am	S.O.S. signals observed & barrage increased. Enemy cruks attacked.	
		5-30am	Situation normal; Enemy repulsed from trenches leaving 93 prisoners.	
		12-6pm	18th Divn Art Operation Order No 26 commenced. 39th Divn is to capture STUFF TRENCH supported by 18th Divn Art. 85th Bde enfilading and searching ground on 82nd 83rd & 84th Ddes R.fr. knots. This operation was successfully carried out and STUFF TRENCH from R.20.c.5.5. to the SCHWABEN REDOUBT is now in our possession. Heavy night firing was maintained in order to harass the enemy.	
—"—	22/10/16	3.6pm to 5.15pm	The villages of MIRAUMONT — BEAUMONT HAMEL — and GRANDCOURT were bombarded by Heavy Artillery. Observation of the fire by F.O.O. reported as very effective. The enemy did not retaliate. Normal Barrage maintained during day	MPH
—"—	23/10/16		Enemy's defences & approaches kept under fire during day & night to prevent them being repaired. Visibility very bad.	MPH
—"—	24/10/16	3pm to 4.15pm	— Do — Wire cutting carried out from R.19.a.0.4. to 5-4, but not completed owing to bad visibility. (Map Ref - ST PIERRE DIVION 1/5000)	MPH

Confidential

Army Form C. 2118

WAR DIARY
or
INTELLIGENCE SUMMARY
(Erase heading not required.)

Instructions regarding War Diaries and Intelligence
Summaries are contained in F.S. Regs., Part II.
and the Staff Manual respectively. Title Pages
will be prepared in manuscript.

Place	Date	Hour	Summary of Events and Information	Remarks and references to Appendices
MESNIL	25/10/16	9am 1pm 1pm to 4pm	Wire cutting continued from R.19.a.04 to 5.4 and reported completely destroyed except 4 yds at R.19.a.24. Battery Comdrs assisted the 4th & 7th R.H.O Btys to nights. These Brigades having just come into action. A/85 detailed to fire on cut wire during night to prevent enemy repairing same	MH
----	26/10/16	6 am to 7 am	2/Lt. S.F.T REES A/85 posted attached to Trench Mortar Battery. 2/Lt. F.H LEMON (I.F.A.A.C) attached to A/85 for course of Instruction. Slow barrage put up on night lines, owing to enemy heavily shelling the night sector. (The SCHWABEN REDOUBT.) Normal Barrage Maintained remainder of day	MH
----	27/10/16	12.30 pm	Wire cutting continued & completed. 16th Rifle Bde relieved the 16th NOTTS & DERBYS Btn Normal Barrage maintained during day.	MH
----	28/10/16 29 30 31		Normal Barrage Maintained. Enemy defences kept under fire to prevent repair of same, during night & day.	MH

M.H House Lt. & Adjt.
for, O.C. 85/Bde R.F.A

War Diary
for
November 1916

85th Bde. R.F.A.

Confidential

War Diary

25th Infantry Bde "A"

Nov. 1.11.16   to   3.12.16

Vol XI

Army Form. C. 2118.

Confidential

WAR DIARY
or
INTELLIGENCE SUMMARY.

(Erase heading not required.)

Instructions regarding War Diaries and Intelligence Summaries are contained in F.S. Regs., Part II. and the Staff Manual respectively. Title pages will be prepared in manuscript.

Place	Date	Hour	Summary of Events and Information	Remarks and references to Appendices
MESNIL	1/7/16		Enemy's defences kept under bursts of fire in Q24b-4d also S13 to prevent repair to same being carried out. Wire cutting carried out by A/85 from Q24b-35·10 to 15·10 (Map Ref Beaumont town) 2/Lt R.T. Rowbotham } Posted from R.A.C. to A/85 Respectively. 2/Lt D.T. Pearson } 3/85	MHH
-do-	2/7/16	10 am	A/85 continued wire cutting. Several large gaps observed.	MHH
		11 am to 11·30 am	Enemy heavily shelled Schwaben Redoubt. Gun No 945 condemned by I.O.M.	
-do-	3/7/16	12·2 pm 4·4 pm	Wireless Call received. Infantry at R13 d 3·4 } Both targets were engaged. " " " " R2 b 2·2 }	MHH
		4·30	Schwaben Redoubt & Thiepval Wood shelled very heavily	
		5 pm	117 Infy Bde relieves 118 Infy Bde. 85th Bde now supporting the 16th Bn. Northum Fus	
-do-	4/7/16		Beaumont Hamel & Thiepval slightly shelled during day Operation Order No 99 indefinitely postponed.	MHH
-do-	5/7/16	11 am	A/85 continued wire cutting in Q24b- 35·10, & reported completely cut at 4 pm	MHH
		5 pm	116th Infy Bde relieved 117th Infy Bde. 85 th Bde now supporting 116th Bde Right Divisn	
		6 pm	2/Lt A.S. Robertson I.F.D.A.C. attached to B/85 for course of Instruction.	

Army Form C. 2118.

Confidential

WAR DIARY
or
INTELLIGENCE SUMMARY.

(Erase heading not required.)

Instructions regarding War Diaries and Intelligence Summaries are contained in F. S. Regs. Part II. and the Staff Manual respectively. Title pages will be prepared in manuscript.

Place	Date	Hour	Summary of Events and Information	Remarks and references to Appendices
MESNIL	6/11/16	5 pm	2/Lt T.W. Berry 18 D.A.C. attached to A/85 for duties of Instruction. Enemy heavily shelled Schwaben Redoubt. Fell 6 pm. # 117th I/Fy Bde relieved 116 I/Fy Bde, 85th Bde now supporting 18th Bde. No Stationary. Enemy defences kept under shell fire during hours of darkness. The Hay ration reduced to scale of 8lb per animal.	MPH
-do-	7/11/16	6 pm	Enemy Objectives seen engaged during day & their defences kept under shell fire during hours of darkness. Enemy dropped 5.9 shells round the village of Mesnil till 7 pm.	MPH
-do-	8th	7.30 pm 8 pm	Wagon lines of 85th Bde shelled, no casualties reported. 118th I/Fy Bde relieved 117th I/Fy Bde, 85th Bde now supporting 1/1 Herts Bn. Night firing stopped till further orders and ammunition expenditure reduced to 48 Rds per Battery.	MPH
-do-	9th	10 am	Enemy Aeroplanes active over MESNIL MARTINSART and AVELUY. Rounds of fire were put on a few enemy targets (Infy) in square R.13.d.	MPH
-do-	10th	12 noon	116th I/Fy Bde relieved 118th I/Fy Bde, 85th now supporting 12th Bn. Royal Sussex. Wire cutting resumed from R.19.a.04 to 5.4, also from Q.24.b.15.05 to 0.1. most of this wire was cut. Night firing resumed on enemy's defences.	MPH

A 5834 Wt. W4973/M687 750,000 8/16 D.D. & L. Ltd. Forms/C.2118/13.

Army Form C. 2118.

WAR DIARY
or
INTELLIGENCE SUMMARY.
(Erase heading not required.)

Place	Date	Hour	Summary of Events and Information	Remarks and references to Appendices
MESNIL	11/11/16	5.45 am to 5.52 am	An intense bombardment was carried out in the nature of a barrage with a lift & return to first objective with a view to deceiving the enemy on day of attack. This caused suspected owing to bad visibility Enemy's defences are kept under obs'n this day & night.	MH
do	12/11/16	5.4.5am to 5.52 am	Bombardment carried out similar to yesterday. Enemy's retaliation was very feeble.	MH
	10 am		Wire cutting carried out by A/95 from 8.24 to 15.15 to 00.15 & destroyed. Night firing increased to 75 Rds Per Bde Per Hour.	
do	13/11/16	5.45 am	Operation Order 99 commenced, with a view to capturing the line Piccot R.13.t.3.5. R.134.9t.95. The 39th Div'n will attack at dawn supported by 18th Div'n Art'y. 85th supporting in Barrage work in accordance with programme.	MH
	8.50 am		All objectives south of River Ancre had been captured, including about 1500 prisoners.	
	10 am		85th are ordered to enfilade HANSA Rd to GRANDCOURT from R.14.07 to Village as a hostile barrage.	

Army Form C. 2118.

WAR DIARY
or
INTELLIGENCE SUMMARY.
(Erase heading not required.)

Place	Date	Hour	Summary of Events and Information	Remarks and references to Appendices
MESNIL	13/7/16	contd	The Bde was kept in this line for S.O.S purposes, also for night firing. Night firing 16 Rds Per Battery Per hour.	N/A H
		8pm	118 Infy Bde Hd Qrs being moved to St PIERRE DIVION, telephone communication was established, but owing to enemy's barrage this line could not be used during the night. The 118 Infy Bde Hd Qrs moved back to PAISLEY DUMP.	N/A H
-Do-	14/7/16	6 a.m.	The 63rd Divis on left flank continued situations at 6 a.m.	
		10 a.m.	Telephone communication now established to St PIERRE Divion 118 Infy Bde Hd Qrs in German Dug outs captured yesterday. R.13.c.5.9. 85th MGC supporting 117 Infy Regt. Hd Qrs at R.13.c.5.9.	N/A H
-Do-	15/7/16	3.45 am	Left Infy Bn moved to 8.24 to 8.7; 55 Bde now supporting 9th Royal Lancs 19th D.W.R:	
		5.45 8.50 4.12 to 5.50	Enemy heavily shelled HANZA LINE. Retaliation was carried out by 93rd Bde during that period. Enemy did not make any Counter attack. -Do-	N/A H

Confidential

Army Form C. 2118.

WAR DIARY
or
INTELLIGENCE SUMMARY.

(Erase heading not required.)

Instructions regarding War Diaries and Intelligence Summaries are contained in F.S. Regs., Part II. and the Staff Manual respectively. Title pages will be prepared in manuscript.

Place	Date	Hour	Summary of Events and Information	Remarks and references to Appendices
MESNIL	16/11/16	1 pm	85th Bde Front redistributed for Protective Barrage. R.P.C. 50 L.P. & a 5.3./ (Map Ref. Beaumont 1/10000.)	MH
		2 pm	C/85 registered GRANDCOURT TRENCH, WRETCHED WAY.	
		9.30 pm to 11 pm	Gas alert received owing to report that gas was coming on P20 a & b.	
— do —	17th Nov	9 am	B/85 established an O.P. at Q.18.a.3.2. to obtain a better view of GRANDCOURT & country.	NHH
		4.30 & 9.30 am	85th 13th Barrage Targets redistributed as under:- P.P.C. 50 to R.P.C. 53 & also enfilade the HANZA Rd to GRANDCOURT VILLAGE.	
— do —	18th	7 am	Liaison Officer 85th Bde was detailed to report to the 7th St Loues attacking battalion of 56th Infy Bde 19 Divn. Communication was established by same.	
		6.10 am	Operation Order No. 104 commenced. 19th Divn will attack GRANDCOURT TRENCH & GRANDCOURT in conjunction with 18th Divn. 2nd by 5th Corps on the PUISIEUX Trench, & BAILLESCOURT. The attack will be supported by 17-18-19 th Divn L Art. 85th Bde supported attack by enfilading in front of the Frontal Barrage of the other Bdes.	NHH
		5 pm	The situation as a result of to-day's operations still remains somewhat doubtful. The objectives of the 17th Regn 17 (9th) Divn are reported to have been captured. Main objective	

Army Form C. 2118.

Confidential

WAR DIARY
or
INTELLIGENCE SUMMARY.
(Erase heading not required.)

Instructions regarding War Diaries and Intelligence Summaries are contained in F.S. Regs., Part II. and the Staff Manual respectively. Title pages will be prepared in manuscript.

Place	Date	Hour	Summary of Events and Information	Remarks and references to Appendices
MESNIL	18th Cont		85th Bde moved to establish a protective barrage around the outskirts of EPANCOURT with a view to isolating the village in the event of an attack. Barrage Pq.0.3 to Pq.C.85. (75th Rg: Beaumont) for night firing. About 200 prisoners were reported to have been captured during the division.	WH
—do—	19th	5 am	Enemy attacked a strong point at R8.d.4.3, but were repulsed by machine & rifle fire.	WH
		5 hr	Night firing was shopped to 6 Bde Fd Battery Pr Avr. 9.t.5 covering the Pr. Line. In addition to maintain all the line withdrawal of troops from O.G.1 in R8.d & R.14.t also southern extremity of Pusieux Trench also affected during the night.	
—do—	20th		Readjustment of front line on withdrawal from O.G.1 extends as under:— a strong line of Posts connected by continuous trench from R8.C.35–2.5 to western Bank of Battery VALLEY R.u.d.05.60 to R.14.C.65.00.	WH
		9 am	85th Bde Barrage front redistributed in consequence Pq.a.21 to Pq.t.0.3.	
		2 pm	Rifle registered new line to be taken over at 12 am tomorrow.	

Army Form C. 2118.

WAR DIARY
or
INTELLIGENCE SUMMARY.
(Erase heading not required.)

Instructions regarding War Diaries and Intelligence Summaries are contained in F.S. Regs., Part II. and the Staff Manual respectively. Title pages will be prepared in manuscript.

Confidential

Place	Date	Hour	Summary of Events and Information	Remarks and references to Appendices
MESNIL	21st	9am	Bde retired to put over 8 salvos per hour on WRETCHED WAY, during the day.	MH
		12noon	85th Bde Pistache Barrage front redistributed as under:- Pub 37. to R 8 d 2.6.	
		4.45	Enemy heavily shelled front line. Retaliation was ordered, this was increased to SOS Rate at 5.5 pm. At 6 pm the situation was normal, enemy did not attempt to counter attack. Night firing was not carried out.	
-do-	22nd		3rd Infy Bde relieved the 56th Infy Bde in the line, the 85th Bde was supporting the 9th Sherwood Foresters Bn.	MH
-do-	23rd		2nd Lt A.G. Robertson attached from D.A.C. posted to 83rd Bde R.F.A. 2nd Lt N.O. Fletcher joined from Base & posted to B/85.	
		3.35 p.	Battery Bihans on Mesnil Ridge shelled by Pack Howitzers. Retaliation was carried out by shelling GRANDCOURT for 20 minutes. Night firing was carried out on the main St in GRANDCOURT.	MH

Confidential

Army Form C. 2118.

WAR DIARY
or
INTELLIGENCE SUMMARY.
(Erase heading not required.)

Place	Date	Hour	Summary of Events and Information	Remarks and references to Appendices
MESNIL	24th		2/Lt R Robertson posted from A/85 to C/85. Orders received today that on withdrawal from the line the 18th D.A. will be reformed into 6 Gun Batteries, the following sections of 85th Bde Arty Bde being as under:— Right Section A/85 to A/82; Rt. Sec. B/85 to B/83; Rt. Sec. C/85 to B/82; L.S. B/85 to C/83; L.S. C/85 to A/83. Left " A/85	MWH
		4pm	Capt C W Crumplin admitted to Hospital.	
-do-	25th	11am	Mesnil shelled with 10.5 cm shells. Night firing carried out on GRANDCOURT MAIN STREET. Visibility very bad.	MWH
-do-	26th		Observation very bad. Night firing was reduced to 20 Rds Per Bde. Pr. Bde.	MWH
-do-	27th	12.15am	Retaliation carried out on O.G.1 in reply to enemy shelling front line.	MWH
		11.15am	-do-	MWH
-do-	28th		A & B Batteries commenced building new Gun Platforms ready to move to forward position near C/85 in view of future operation.	MWH

Confidential

Army Form C. 2118.

WAR DIARY
or
INTELLIGENCE SUMMARY.
(Erase heading not required.)

Instructions regarding War Diaries and Intelligence Summaries are contained in F.S. Regs., Part II. and the Staff Manual respectively. Title pages will be prepared in manuscript.

Place	Date	Hour	Summary of Events and Information	Remarks and references to Appendices
MESNIL	3/12/16	10 am	18th Divn Artillery being this day reorganised into 6 Gun Batteries the 83rd Batteries & Hd Qrs were broken up & allotted to other Brigades as under:—	MH
			2/Lt R.F. 7 Bat Lt. Hope Johnstone, O.C. attached 15 Bn S.T.	
			Lieut & Adjt W. Witham to F 2nd Bde. R.F.A.	
			Lieut W.J. Wilson to 83rd Bde R.F.A.	
			Capt J.O. Back Rance to 18th D.A.C.	
			2/Lt J. O'Connor Ave to 18 D.A.C.	
			Capt L.O. Crawfiw to 84th Bde R.F.A.	
			Capt F.H. Aslatt to 83rd Bde R.F.A.	
			Capt M.H. Paterson to 84th/73 Bde R.F.A.	
			Lieut T. Burry } to 83rd Bde R.F.A.	
			"Lt E.I. Pearson }	
			2/Lt R.F. Rowbotham to 83rd Bde R.F.A.	

Army Form C. 2118.

WAR DIARY
or
INTELLIGENCE SUMMARY.

(Erase heading not required.)

Place	Date	Hour	Summary of Events and Information	Remarks and references to Appendices
MESNIL	29th		2Lt Lemon attached from 1 D.A.C. admitted to hospital. A/75 Battery continued work on new gun platforms.	MH
–do–	30th		Capt O.W. Crumplin A/85 reported to Unit for duty from hospital. Orders received that the Bde will withdraw from the line on the 2nd December 1916.	MH
–do–	1/12		2Lt L.D. Fletcher B/85 posted to A/85. 2Lt Berry A/85 posted to B/85.	MH
		6pm	Defence of the line taken over by 11th Divl Arty. 85th Bde orders not to fire again except in case of an S.O.S. call being received.	MH
–do–	2/12	9am	B/85 withdraws to Wagon line. echelons empty.	
		9.30am	C/85 " " " "	
		10am	A/85 " " " "	
		Noon	All ammunition handed over at Gun line to 11 Divl Art. Bde H.Q. 85 moved to Wagon line.	MH

Confidential

WAR DIARY
or
INTELLIGENCE SUMMARY

Army Form C. 2118.

Place	Date	Hour	Summary of Events and Information	Remarks and references to Appendices
MENSE	3/12/16	cont.	2Lt T.C Barker to 83rd Bde R.F.A.	
			2Lt T.W Berry to 83rd Bde R.F.A.	
			Lt G.L Carroll to 82nd Bde R.F.A.	
			2Lt H.A. Currie to 82nd Bde R.F.A.	
			2Lt H.D Hutton to 18th D.A.C. }	M.H.
			2Lt S.T.F Rees }	
			2Lt G Sormay }	
			Right Section A/85 transferred to A/82 with Guns, Wagons & Personnel.	
			Left " " " C/82 " " " "	
			Right " A/85 " " B/83 " " " "	
			Left " B/85 " " C/83 " " " "	
			Right " C/85 " " B/82 " " " "	
			Left " C/85 " " A/83 " " " "	Ancton Village
				" " " "
				" " " "
				" " " "
				" " " "
				from O.C. 85 Bde R.F.A.
				3-12-16